Revolutionary Blues

MJ Politis, Ph.D., D.V.M.

Long Rider Press
www.longriderpress.net

This book is a work of fiction. Names, characters, places and incidents are either products of the author's imagination or are used fictitiously. Any resemblance to actual events or locales or persons, living or dead, is entirely coincidental.

LONG RIDER BOOKS
Box 78, Monte Creek, BC V0E 2M0 Canada

First edition, August 2002

Printed and bound in Canada

ISBN 1-896629-04-0

Chapter 1

The morning sun rose over the horizon on the battlefield of the Ardenne Forest, attempting to shine some light through the midst. It was only 1916, barely two years after the Great War began, yet the landscape bore witness to a conflict that dragged on for a decade. A once lush forest was reduced to a plain of muddy stubble, which was all too good at nurturing the seeds of human suffering. There seemed to be no shortage of soil to produce the crops of pain, helplessness and despair. Indeed, this was the devil's heartland, upon which suffering could go on forever and thwart the natural delivery of death.

A look into the eyes of the soldiers, both living and dead, gave even the most insensitive observer hard proof that the futile struggle for victory - or even survival - had lasted for at least a century. The dead were at peace, or so the living chose to believe.

An expatriate American in a British officer's uniform, with well developed muscles distributed around his perfectly proportioned Herculean body, woke up early that morning. Unlike his native country, Charlie O'Brien had been involved in the Great War since its beginning. He would gladly die to save any one of his men, yet after each battle, it was those privates and corporals who lay dead or wounded, and it was Charlie who emerged without a scratch.

Charlie looked over the long trenches of soldiers emerging from yet another night of restless sleep. He moved to a spot as isolated from human suffering and human companionship as he could, so that he could perhaps make sense of the day which was about to come.

Charlie remembered when the Ardenne Forest was a forest, teeming with life. This time of the day was particularly alive then. The rising of the sun would be nature's cue for all the animals in the forest to sing songs of their own composition, resulting in a symphony more beautiful than any that could be composed by the hand of man. As the final coda came to a close, there would be a total silence: a communal prayer from life to its Creator. Then the miracle of another day would begin, full of surprises that challenged the spirit but did not break the heart. The forest air in those times somehow smelled freshest at that magical hour of the day.

The trees and animals were gone now. The smell of wonderment was replaced by the stench of rotted flesh from dead carcasses and the decaying toes of soldiers with trench foot. Charlie knew that the disease was caused by bacterial decay, small microbes easily killed by all-too-scarce medical supplies. To those afflicted, it was more deadly than any German bullet.

A run or even a hobble home would be the best cure, yet this was not an option. The high command in the back-line villas was very good at convincing their men in the trenches that desertion was cowardice. To ensure esprit d'corp, the French military police were everywhere, their bullets seldom missing the backs of fleeing deserters.

Charlie took a pouch of tobacco from his pocket and rolled himself a cigarette. Its shape was that of the OB-446 torpedo, designed by him in 1905. The OB-446 was originally intended to transport medical supplies between ships during squalls and hurricanes. A small number were made. Fewer were used. By 1914, generals were very effective in dictating scientific priorities to civilian politicians. The British found that OB-446 torpedoes were deadly against German supply ships when attached to any kind of explosive. The Germans were fast to duplicate the innovative design. Both sides honored its original inventor.

Charlie took out his last three matches. They were still firm and dry, not yet dampened by the stagnant trench water that permeated everyone and everything. He struck the matchsticks hard and firm, with skill and determination. Small victories were essential in large stalemates, and Charlie was determined to keep his tobacco away from the rats, and the matches away from the elements. Each flick of Charlie's match was answered with a burst of wind from the treeless landscape, extinguishing each in turn. The bolder he struck, the harder the wind. Most *curry mornings* he could outguess the wind, but not today.

He reluctantly reached into his pocket and pulled out a gold lighter. On it an inscription, "Happy Birthday, Charlie, from your commanding officer and friend, L.L. Wentworth." Charlie gazed at it reflectively, then flicked the lighter. The flame came up tall and stood up boldly against the oncoming wind. Charlie hesitated. He found his hand moving closer to the cigarette tip. He went into a trance.

"Sir...Major O'Brien," said a young Scottish Lieutenant, in a quiet, compassionate voice that came from a wrinkleless face miraculously not hardened by war.

"?" Charlie replied with a reverence for sloppy diction consistent with his American heritage.

"The men. They're ready," replied the Lieutenant.

Charlie put away his unlit cigarette and walked with the Lieutenant toward the observation post. His eyes remained fixed on the lighter, oblivious to everything else around him. Charlie knew that all human misery was somehow hooked onto that gold lighter and to his reflection in it. He was sure of this. He also knew that no one would believe him if he said why this was so. It was a divinely designed punishment.

They passed a long line of men loading their rifles and cleaning the mud out of the short range artillery that bore the "OB" mark, after its expatriate American inventor. "You prepared the men well. We'll win this one for sure," commented the Lieutenant.

"Yeah," Charlie said, hoping that the Lieutenant would be right, but knowing that he wasn't.

"Maybe today we'll end this stinkin' war altogether. So we can ALL go home. Them and us." The Lieutenant continued gazing at the German lines, just visible over the fog clearing up, right on schedule.

"Yeah," replied Charlie, with a small smile shown but not felt. He gave the lighter to the Lieutenant. "Happy Birthday," he said with as much optimism as he could muster.

"It's not my birthday. And you've had this for as long as I've known you, since this thing started," the Lieutenant answered, puzzled.

"Happy birthday, Lieutenant," Charlie repeated. He forced his head up and moved on, with a bold stride befitting his appointed rank and station.

The whistle blew, signaling the men to their daily work of being slaughtered. A mass of British soldiers poured out of their trenches on the offensive, giving out a loud battle cry that clouded both fear and reason. The German command countered with an offensive charge of its own.

Metal clashed with metal on the scorched earth. Flesh was ripped apart in its wake. Everything was chaos - very deadly chaos. Then there came the sound of certainty from the trench guns. Artillery shells from both sides decimated whatever life was left on the field, as if by mutual consent.

Charlie looked on from his observation deck, powerless to stop it.

Powerless, helpless, and responsible. The nightmare took on more absurd proportions when he heard applause. From out of the black smoke blanketing the battleground emerged a spectacle even more horrifying than Charlie had ever witnessed even in the worst of his nightmares.

High ranking officers and politicians, representing all countries involved in the Great War, came onto the field in full regalia, applauding the players who lay dead at their feet. Blindfolded waiters served red wine to the dignitaries from the detached limbs of soldiers who had made the ultimate sacrifice for King and Country. A marching band appeared, garbed in the finest uniforms available from the factories of London, Paris and Berlin. Their music was loud and boisterous and full of pride, played with an enthusiastic two-four time that demanded, rather than requested, the listener's attention.

Then, from the blackened mist to the East, emerged a tall man with cold, hard chiseled features. His uniform was spotless. The medals on his chest absorbed the sunlight and converted it to well defined beams that blinded the observer. His footsteps echoed like thunder, but his bootheels left no footprints on the blood-soaked ground.

The ominous figure walked to a central point on the festival ground. The earth rose up from below his feet, raising him above the eyes of all in the crowd. The marching band stopped playing. Then, silence. Then, "God Save the King."

The officers took off their helmets. The politicians removed their top hats. The music echoed in the midst, like a distorted prayer delivered to the wrong deity by the most devoted of subjects.

All heads were bowed to Wentworth, except Charlie's. The world knew this demagogue as Lord Wentworth, a powerful industrialist who had more influence than any Prime Minister, King, Kaiser or, for that matter, any other earthly ruler. Charlie knew who and what Wentworth really was. But contrary to what had been taught in the gold-laden churches owned by Wentworth, the truth did NOT set one free. Wentworth had absolute power here, and he would not be brought down by anything so trivial as "truth." This war was good for business, particularly Wentworth's business.

Charlie screamed out to the living, then the dead, begging them to leave the orchestrated madness glorified by the euphemism of war. This was clearly not the war to end all wars, but one which would ensure the perpetuation of that deadly, though profitable, enterprise.

Even the Scottish Lieutenant had his head bowed to Wentworth as the music played on. A bowed head conferred blindness to the worshipper, and the music demanded that heads be bowed.

It was a powerful piece of manipulation, "God Save the King" appreciated. Beethoven used it to rouse internationalist emotions in his dedication to Wellington's victory over Napoleon. The rebellious American Republic was quick to keep the tune, changing the lyrics to "My Country 'Tis of Thee." "God Save the King" had inspired Charlie in his youth and pre-cynical adulthood. It drove terror into his heart now. But part of him still stood at attention, even as he screamed out, begging for it to stop.

Finally the music ended. Hats and helmets went on heads filled with glory but depleted of judgment. A Captain stood up and announced in a loud and bold voice, "Gentlemen, His Excellency Lord Wentworth."

The crowd burst into applause. Wentworth lifted up his hand, slightly. He gave a condescending smile. Even the lowest private in the crowd felt like in.

Charlie's mind screamed "No, don't listen to him." His mouth could not utter a sound. The words were held hostage by his conscience. Charlie tried to run toward Wentworth to silence him with his bare hands, but he couldn't move. His boots were glued to the ground by red ooze coming out of the mud below his feet.

Wentworth commenced, in an Oxford accent spoken with deadly precision, "Today is a special day. For today we honor accomplishment, tradition, and a very special man. A man without whom today's festival of superiority would not have been possible."

The crowd applauded again, wildly. Charlie screamed, "No, it's not true," but his words fell on the deafest of ears.

Wentworth continued, a proud smile on his face. "We have among us a man who I consider like a son, and whose contribution to our way of life has been immeasurable."

Bodies of soldiers who had fallen in battle came to life and stood at attention. Freshly polished tanks, artillery, and transport vehicles of all kinds were brought on to the battlefield and wheeled around in a choreographed display.

"No," Charlie screamed even louder. "I'm innocent. I was tricked. I was tricked."

Wentworth continued, "The visionary who created these technological miracles belongs among our ranks." The ovation was loud enough to be heard across the world. It was a proud day for Lord Wentworth. Perhaps his finest hour.

Charlie screeched out at the top of his lungs, "You told me it wouldn't be like this!!! You told me it wouldn't be like this!!!." He turned to the Scottish Lieutenant. "This was supposed to be a war to end all wars. Wentworth promised me that. He promised me that it was supposed to...."

Charlie gasped. The Lieutenant had been wounded near the heart, bright red blood streaming out of his chest. In the center of it, the lighter Charlie had given him just minutes earlier, Wentworth's inscription on it more visible than ever.

The crowd got louder, running drunker with ignorance. With each cheer, another spurt of blood from the young Lieutenant's heart, and another knife through Charlie's tortured soul. Charlie grabbed the lighter, but it was embedded deep in the young man's chest. It burned hotter than fire itself, though the flesh around it was cold as ice.

Charlie went at it again, grabbing the lighter he once valued so much, with the sole objective of destroying it so it would not take another victim. It would take the courage of a fierce lion this time, not the hands of a skilled surgeon. To make matters worse, the lighter was getting longer and more torturous by the second, creeping its way into the Lieutenant's body like a rapid snake.

Charlie could smell his own flesh burn as he pulled the tail of the serpentine lighter with all his might, maneuvering it around the chest wall and between two broken ribs with whatever anatomy knowledge his hands could retain. The Lieutenant's face turned pale and ghostlike. The ribs collapsed around the lighter, securing it in place like cooling lava. Charlie closed his eyes, screamed out a prayer of defiance, and pulled with all his might.

Only two seconds passed, but it seemed like a lifetime. Charlie's tenacity hurled him into another dimension. He found himself on the ground, the lighter next to him, burning the residual flesh of a rat down to the bone. He grabbed a metal hammer which was so conveniently present and pounded the lighter. He only succeeded in mutilating the rodent's dying body. The lighter remained. His hands were roasted, the pain of the third degree burns penetrating up his arms and into his tormented mind. But the stream of blood from the Lieutenant's chest stopped. Color miraculously came to his body, but still no breath in it. Charlie breathed his own into the Lieutenant as hard as he could, hoping that desperation could change the inevitable laws of cause and effect that dictated his own doom, and the death of those around him.

Suddenly, the Lieutenant started to breathe on his own. Charlie sat back, feeling enough strength in his young friend's carotid pulse to trust that nature could take over. Finally, relief. A small victory and contentment. Barely a moment later, a black cloud came over the Lieutenant's body, leaving a lifeless skeleton in its wake. Then nothing. It was always like that. Death taking its toll in one moment, leaving Charlie an eternity of moments to relive it. Maybe if Charlie had taken the time to know Lieutenant John McGregor by name instead of rank, station or function, he could have saved him. Maybe not.

"Enough," Charlie shouted at Wentworth's display a few hundred yards to the east. He pulled his feet out of his boots and ran westward as fast as he could, hoping that it would somehow lead home. No one noticed, which was both a blessing and a curse.

"And so," Wentworth continued, "It is my honor and privilege to introduce to you, General Charlie O'Brien." He turned to Charlie's observation post to find it empty. Wentworth's face turned beet red with anger, and a subtly delivered flick of his finger sent the Captain off in search of the honored guest.

"Where's Charlie? We want Charlie." someone in the crowd asked. The congregation joined in. "We want Charlie, we want Charlie."

Wentworth's anger was fueled by the embarrassment of losing his star prodigy. Charlie was like a son to him. Wentworth had gotten Charlie into university and arranged things so that his mental tenacity could be turned into genius, both in science and politics. Wentworth's influence as an administrator of the Industrial Age gave Charlie the clout to grab the spotlight - something Charlie always wanted since he was a boy growing up in his uncle's house in Albany, New York. Albany was a pleasant place to grow up, for most of its residents. But for Charlie it was boring, and Charlie would do anything to avoid boredom. Wentworth was all too eager to grant that wish. There were times when "love" described what was going on between Charlie and Wentworth. But it was a love based in mutual need and privately kept agendas on both sides.

The Captain came back to Wentworth empty-handed and shivering in his boots. The crowd demanded that the festival continue as scheduled. "What have you to report, Captain?" requested Wentworth, as he wavered between shedding a tear in regret and clenching his fist in vengeful anger.

"Major O'Brien is nowhere to be found, Sir," the Captain announced loudly. He stood rigidly at attention, praying that he would not be punished for being the bearer of such unexpected news.

Charlie had broken the chain of command by refusing to be one of its links. Wentworth was enraged, but held in his anger. He had to maintain the illusion of being in control. The crowd became bewildered, then frightened. A world without chains was the scariest thing imaginable to officers and enlisted alike.

Wentworth had to act - quickly and with a single-minded purpose. He unleashed his rage and disappointment in a loud cry, commanding all available men to retrieve Charlie at any cost.

Charlie ran westward across trenches and scorched battlefields as fast as he could, peeling off his uniform enroute. He could feel the cold north wind penetrate his body, exposing his soul to the raw elements for the first time in years. It was painful, but Charlie needed some harsh pain to ease his spiritual suffering.

As he got further from the battlefield the earth became brown, then once again green. The blistering North wind gave way to warm gentle breezes from the ocean that lay just over the next hill.

Charlie kept running for what seemed like an endless climb up a treeless slope. Then, at the top of the hill, lay the big waters of the Atlantic. Beyond those waters was the Western horizon. Somewhere on the other side of that horizon there was a world Charlie knew before the war, in Sonora, Mexico.

A vision of those golden times appeared to him in the waters below the steep cliff. A canoe made with a bamboo frame. Guiding the craft through the rocky coastal waters stood a Yaqui Indian curandero shaman, bare to the waist, wearing a deerskin belt and cocoon-rattler anklets. He had a gentle smile, framed by wrinkles that penetrated deeply into his sunbaked face.

The curandero waved to Charlie, beckoning him to jump off the cliff into the waters 400 feet below. Anticipating the fear anyone would have of such a jump, he pointed to his companion in the canoe to give Charlie extra encouragement.

It was a young woman, with a Native heart and a universal soul, named Diane Santa Anna-McFearson, the woman with whom Charlie shared his golden years in Mexico before he signed on to fight the Great War in Europe.

After being taken from her Yaqui mountain village at an early age, Diane was placed under the care of a Scottish-owned plantation in the Yucatan. Her small nose, chiseled jaw and narrow hips made her unattractive by Yaqui standards, but very desirable to John McFearson. Lord McFearson, as he was called everywhere in Mexico, but never in his native Scotland, saw it as his sacred duty to help the "inferior races" by integrating them into the superior ones. For reasons no one except Diane knew, John McFearson saw to it that no expense was spared in her education. She crossed Charlie's path at Yale, where they instantly became traveling companions, each giving the other the courage to hit the road with grit and gusto.

During that golden time of invincibility, Charlie's passions were firmly entrenched in medicine, and his aspirations not yet corrupted by politics. Both Diane and Charlie saw the inadequacies of science in the industrialized world, and the vast potential of its humane application in the third world. A mutually agreed upon mission of self discovery led the pair to Mexico, Sonora, and then to the Yaqui.

That time in the northwestern Mexican desert was perhaps the only period when Charlie experienced real happiness. The Indians gave him a heritage he could believe in, and a belief in Christ which did not demand surrender of dignity or destruction of mother nature for salvation. Diane offered herself as a real friend, ally, and lover, all at the same time. Such were the demands of loners like Charlie, who were born to make their mark on the world but to never live in it.

Charlie could go back to 1907 Sonora with a single jump off the French cliffs to the canoe below. But he hesitated. Perhaps it was the fear of being torn to shreds by the trees lining the cliff. Perhaps it was the fear of smashing onto the jagged rocks inches below the choppy waters. Perhaps it was the fear of finding out that he would sink the boat if he accepted the offer of these good friends to go home. Perhaps there was no home to come back to at all, and these two comrades from the past were as lost as he was.

Charlie's fear was intensified by indecision, and then panic. Behind him were the transport vehicles he designed, in hot pursuit, eager to take him back to the Great War and Lord Wentworth. All that would be required to have his sin of insolence erased clean would be an apology - a surrender of dignity. Dignity was a valueless currency in Wentworth's world. Besides, Charlie had not felt anything close to dignity in a long time.

The curandero waved his hand again, begging Charlie to break away from the world that had betrayed him. But fear still kept Charlie's judgment hostage. His lips quivered, his legs rigidly locked in place.

The curandero's smile turned downward, disappointed and silently angry. He would go the distance for Charlie, but the American expatriate would have to make the first step.

Diane made that step possible, as she had done so many times before in so many ways. She outstretched her arms like a Madonna, more pure and virgin that any that could have been created by white Christianity. Charlie's shackles to death disintegrated as the light of Diane's warmth penetrated his cold heart, and her passion breathed fire into his tired soul. He took a deep breath and took the plunge, smiling, as he trusted gravity to pull him down to the canoe and up into the heavens.

Echoing in Charlie's ears was Diane's voice gently calling his name and the scent of Mexican sagebrush penetrated into his nostrils, filling his head with the smell of wonderment. Charlie's eyes were closed, but his heart was wide open. His fingertips felt Diane's touch. Time slowed down, and every second felt like a lifetime.

The warmth of Diane's hand melted the fog of bitterness that held his heart hostage for the better part of a decade. Her reassuring grasp of his hand turned his lips upward into a smile that felt awkward to his weather-beaten face. Her lips pressing against his hands instantly cured the third degree burns made by Wentworth's serpent lighter, and sealed up the cuts inflicted by OB-1454A barbed wire.

Finally, he breathed a sigh of relief. He prepared himself to wake up a lifetime away. Then a special type of pain he had never experienced.

Charlie opened his eyes. Around his chest was a rope. Attached to the other side, an O'Brien prototype helicopter pulling him up to the top of the cliff. Diane tossed up a shell, its razor edge sharp enough to cut the rope. She pleaded to Charlie to let go. Charlie tried to cut the rope, his hand trembling with fear. The more he shook, the more the shell lost its edge, until it disintegrated in his hand. Charlie screamed out Diane's name, desperately reaching out his blood-soaked hand. It was decided. The curandero could only watch.

The offshore swells shifted the tide, pulling the canoe out to sea. The curandero used whatever power he had left to stop the boat from tipping over. He feared that this long journey would come to this. He was used to disappointment, but never found a way to not feel the pain it brought him. Diane would have to be returned home, and he was needed elsewhere.

The chopper dropped Charlie on top of the cliff, cracking his back and leaving him looking up helplessly at the graying sky above. Aimed at his head, ten guns.

"Do it, damn it. Do it already!!!," Charlie cried out, blinding himself from the faces of his executioners, his arrogance taken over by fear.

"Ready, aim," began the head executioner in a stern British accent.

Charlie closed his eyes tightly, repeatedly muttering under his breath, "Jesus...let me, let me in."

Charlie's pleas were answered with laughter. A look upward horrified Charlie more than the fear of any bullet.

They were the skeletons, clad in uniforms from both sides of the war. The ghosts of men who lost their lives because of Charlie's skill as a weapons designer and military strategist. Each wave of terror that went through Charlie's body gave more life to the skeletons. "Jesus, let me in...," Charlie kept repeating.

"We don't think so," replied the representatives of the dead, elected to take revenge upon the living.

The young Scottish Lieutenant was amongst their number, his optimistic trust in humanity since replaced with vengeful sadism, directed at the man who forced him to lose his life and, most importantly, his innocence.

Echo upon echo vibrated through Charlie's ears. He felt a bayonet thrust through his ear drum, twisting like a screw and slowly turning his brilliant mind into mince meat. The once-bold expatriate crumbled up in a fetal position, all dignity lost. It was a prelude to the worst kind of death possible. Then the end finally came.

Chapter 2

When Charlie awoke from this all too familiar nightmare, his mind could still feel France in 1916. His eyes saw the Texas desert in 1925. The big Western sky was clear and blue, with a horizon that gave an inviting definition to the word "infinity." Life came out of the ground in the forms of cactus, sagebrush, and a multitude of other plants, which defiantly broke through the dry rocky soil to embrace the sun itself. The gophers, coyotes and armadillos had a special spark in their eye - a spark that made them seem like the most distant of strangers, yet also the closest of friends.

Charlie deserted the army in 1916, but it took him nearly ten years to make tracks to Mexico. Wentworth did not approve of the journey, nor the activities Charlie had engaged in after he signed his own discharge papers. It would have been logical for Wentworth to let Charlie retreat into the Mexican desert, and for Charlie to let Wentworth control the rest of the world. But logic was not the operative emotion in 1916, and it was never the operative emotion between Charlie and Wentworth.

Charlie's activities after his desertion turned Wentworth's anger into vendetta. There were the antiwar protests in New York, to prevent American blood from being spilled in a slaughter begun and maintained by European royalty. Charlie was particularly good at these peace rallies when they turned into riots.

There were the labor strikes. Charlie found a natural niche as the translator of Marxist doctrine for Canadian and American laborers who were barely literate.

And the news stand where Charlie waged a special kind of warfare. Though one of the best paid "underground" authors, he was also the hardest working, a little appreciated trait amongst his "peers." With every spare thought, he struggled to find magic words to break the curse of ignorance. It was as much an act of dedication as one of penance.

Then there was Emma, Wentworth's daughter. Emma was ten years younger than Charlie, and her soul was centuries fresher. She had an enthusiasm which could not be quenched by reason, hardship or disillusionment. Life was both a passion and a dance to her. Her father's money had given Emma the chance to study journalism and literature at Columbia. Charlie's fire had given her the chance to take her mind out of the classroom, and her perspectives out of her father's world. She made Charlie smile and sometimes even laugh.

Charlie's course of action now put him squarely at the mercy of fate - the cycle of cause and effect which demands retribution, usually when it is least respected. He hoped that salvation lay south of the Rio Grande, in the arms of another woman and another culture. Perhaps he could start again. Perhaps whores such as Charlie could regain their virginity if they worked or prayed hard enough.

But the arm of the law was long, and that law demanded payment in full from Charlie for not fulfilling his contractual agreements with the military-industrial machine. Wentworth's hired killers had the most deadly weapons available. Every bullet had Charlie's name invisibly inscribed on it. By 1925 the expatriate had no safe haven anywhere, except for one place.

Wentworth's edicts and bullets couldn't hurt Charlie once he reached Yaqui territory in Mexico. The intensity of the Yaqui protected them from monsters like Wentworth. It was about more than the unmatched skills of the Yaqui in combat, or their ability to survive in some of the most rugged badlands nature could design. Yaqui intensity came from inner spiritual strength, and even Wentworth was powerless against it. If Charlie could redeem himself from the inside, perhaps he could attain sanctuary amongst these special people in the Yaqui river valley.

That sanctuary was getting closer, yet further away, every day. Wentworth's bounty hunters awaited at every turn of the journey that was taking a more torturous route every day.

The campsite he chose that day was isolated, and beautiful. A freedom-loving man could build a cabin there and live like a king for the rest of his life. Add a freedom-loving woman, and he would live like a god.

But it was time to move on. Charlie gathered his scant belongings and went to a nearby stream to refill his canteen, in preparation for another day's travel through the desert. He knelt down at the water's edge and he saw his distorted reflection in the rippling waves before him. Once again, he pondered the world which he had left behind.

The tragedy of the Great War was far from over. By 1918, at least ten million lay dead in the wake of the war to end all wars. The dreadful influenza epidemic killed millions more, less than a year after the soldiers came home. Stalin had taken a Communist dream in Russia and turned it into a Bolshevik nightmare. The terms of the Armistice had been, as if by intent, laying down the seeds of poverty, unemployment and despair in Italy and Germany. They were already sprouting the toxic weeds of Fascism. The British, French and Americans had forced a peace based on vengeance rather than reason, allowing madmen like Hitler, Mussolini, and Franco to gain support in nations that had formerly spawned spiritual beacons such as Beethoven, Michelangelo, and Cervantes.

Charlie felt that all of this was some kind of retribution, perhaps directed at himself. If Wentworth wasn't a driving force behind it, then he was certainly an eager participant in all of it. But there was also hope. The League of Nations was not yet dead, and the dream of a world where universal compassion, rather than shallow greed, would rule was alive. Often in places where you least expected it to be.

Ghandi was bringing the British Empire to its knees under the banner of universal compassion. Einstein had become the guru for a pacifist movement that could incorporate liberals, conservatives, and those who hated politics all together.

After all, it did make sense. War brought out bravery in many "ordinary" people, and many times even in cowards. But that bravery was reserved for "family." German soldiers bayoneted unarmed English Infantrymen in the defense of women and children in Berlin, Heidelburg or Vienna. British artillerymen blew up trench-fulls of German youths so they would not rape their sisters and wives in London and Glasgow. It was all about putting family first and strangers last.

If all strangers were family, disputes would be settled with reason - perhaps even compassion.

Charlie admired few people, and looked up to even fewer. Einstein was on the top of a very special and short list. He had never met the funny looking man who looked more like a silent movie comic than a brilliant scientist, but perhaps that is what made the relationship between them more special.

Few understood Einstein's science. Most could feel his humanity. He was quick to jump into the realm of politics, and was very effective at convincing the public that compassion, reason, and self-interest were all the same thing. Some called him a "genius," but to Albert a genius was merely someone who ventured into unexplored territory with eyes open. Anyone could do it. It was about bravery, not intelligence. Tenacity, not talent.

Charlie felt close to Einstein that day in the Texas desert. Clearly, the industrialized world was at a critical crossroad. The forces of good and evil were playing very high stakes poker. Charlie was battleweary and wanted to leave the table. Perhaps somewhere in Mexico there was another card game, with a gentler set of rules and a deeper sense of meaning. But getting up from the poker table is far easier than leaving the game.

Charlie broke camp and got on his motorcycle, a handbuilt four-cylinder marvel which he designed to be light, fast and durable over mountain terrain. He blazed yet another convoluted trail through the desert that provided both safety from Wentworth's bounty hunters and smooth riding for himself. By nightfall, it led him to the banks of a creek, euphemistically called a river by Texans in one of the driest years since 1918.

The water was muddy and stagnant. Charlie's eyes saw it as a crystal clear mountain stream. Part of the reason for Charlie's enthusiasm was a sign nailed to a tree on the banks. The paint on it was faded by the sun and wind but the message was clear enough.

"Mexico, one hundred miles," Charlie read aloud to himself with a broad smile on his face. "I hope it's still home when I get there," he continued with a less affirmative tone.

Charlie prepared to cross the river. Then he heard a scream from down stream. He closed his eyes. Maybe it was his imagination. Then another bloodcurdling plea for help. He opened his eyes. The exodus to Sonora would have to be delayed yet one more time. But then again, he was ten years behind schedule already.

Maria Lopez was tied to a tree with a lariat. Her dress was torn to shreds. Her face was bruised, and there were open whip burns on her back and thighs.

The blood-soaked hands of Deputy Lester Halso ripped off the last of her undergarments. "There ya go, Mammacita. We gonna have us a good old time," he screamed in a high pitched piercing voice, with a wide smile revealing a mouth barely half filled with teeth.

"And yer hubby over there can watch," added Deputy Dan Kletman. His laugh was loud as a donkey, and sadistic as any lawman between the Louisiana Bayou and the New Mexican border.

Fernando Lopez lay tied to a nearby tree with a gag in his mouth. The Lopez "ranch" lay barely ten miles South of the Rio Grande. It produced more rocks than any beans or corn in its shaky ten-year-old history. But the Rothberg cattle ranch saw fit to add Fernando's 3 acres to their 50,000. And whatever Mister Rothberg wanted, he got.

Fernando and Maria were hoping to find work in the Texas oil fields. Kletman and Halson volunteered their services as a welcoming committee.

Halson got what he wanted, by asking. Then by taking. Halson loosened his oversized, imitation-silver Rodeo belt buckle and slowly unbuttoned his fly. He boldly displayed his male genitalia to Maria and his eagerness to use it. She flinched, determined to not lose her dignity. She gathered all the strength she could and directed it into a defiant stare.

"Hey," Halson commented. "It ain't polite to look into a Gringo's eyes. Not unless it's real dark and he's been real satisfied."

Halson pushed Maria's head to the side. He moved in closer. Her eyes followed him, like a mirror forcing Halson to see how small a man he really was.

Maria punctuated her defiance with a spit into Halson's face. He wiped the saliva off his mustache and three-day beard. Kletman laughed.

"She's a mean spirited bitch, ain't she?" commented Kletman, as if describing the attributes of a wild horse that was about to be broken by a sharp pair of spurs and a sturdy whip.

Halson took an 1885 Colt 45 out of his 1919 government issue holster and shoved it into Maria's mouth. He was prepared to use it this time. Maria had ten seconds of courage left. Halson had all the time in the world.

From behind the bushes emerged Chief Deputy Percy Juris, a well built, muscular man, clean shaven, with a pale complexion. "Halson, Kletman. This has gone far enough," he said with quiet authority.

Kletman took another swig of the 125 proof confiscated moonshine. "You may be Chief Deputy in town, but out here you ain't no better than the rest of us."

Halson spread out Maria's arms and legs and dragged a comb through her knotted hair. He took off his shirt and boots and then lowered his trousers. "There is a proper and improper way to rape a woman, even a Mexican bitch," he related.

"Ride 'em cowboy," Kletman yelped. He lifted the jug up and dumped a pint of whiskey down his throat, swallowing as fast as he poured.

Juris was raised Texan, but never belonged anywhere West of the Appalachians. His boyhood companions were books, not people, and the consequences of such a background haunted him into adulthood. The louder he protested, the more he was ignored.

Halson squeezed Maria's breasts, slowly but surely working his way to the big pay-off. He was going to make her enjoy it - a personal challenge. "Juris. Why don't you watch. Learn how a real man is supposed to fuck."

"And what gender yer supposed ta get yer pleasure from," added Kletman.

Juris pointed his revolver at Halson and ordered him to cease his activities, but to no avail. The hands of the Chief Deputy shook, and sweat dripped from his forehead.

"Hey Halson," Kletman added. "Maybe we should let Juris here have a poke at this bitch's hubby over there. I hear that he's real good at that sorta thing."

"That's not true," Juris blurted out, a beat too quickly. "It's all lies."

"Folks believe what they's told, not what they see," countered Kletman. "Besides, ya can prove yer manhood right here, tonight. Ya can have a poke at Mammacita here after Halson's done. Hell, ya can even take my turn. Me and Halson can be witnesses."

Juris had enough. He grabbed Halson by the bandanna around his neck and pulled him off Maria. A twist of his hand could have ended Halson's career as a braggart.

Juris was a reasonable man. Kletman wasn't, and demonstrated it with a firm insertion of his 30-30 Winchester into Juris' back.

"Ya wait yer turn, like a gentleman," Kletman said. He laughed, then drank. Juris felt the pain of helplessness yet again.

Suddenly a voice from an unobserved visitor in the bush. "Hello."

A stranger lurking in the bushes reminded the three lawmen that they still were a "family," and family comes first. Halson grabbed his gun, prepared to use it for survival rather than intimidation. Keltman cocked the lever on his Winchester in a loud and firm motion. Juris let the barrel of his revolver move to and fro, hoping that it would smell out the location of the unseen intruder.

Charlie calmly emerged behind the trio, walking his motorcycle. He parked it in the middle of the camp, sat down at the campfire, and helped himself to a cup of java. "Good coffee," he commented casually, as his startled hosts pointed their guns at his head.

Halson cocked the trigger on his pistol and grunted. "You got five seconds to..."

"How much do you want for the Mexicans?" Charlie interrupted, still calm and still in control from the center of his madness.

In Juris' eyes, Charlie had exceptional courage or incredible stupidity. Either way he would be very dangerous.

"The Mexicans are not for sale," Juris commented.

"Shit, everything's for sale," Kletman interrupted. The chance to pick up some extra money from the stranger before blowing him away intrigued him. "Right, Percy," he continued in an imitative lisp meant to intimidate Juris in the presence of the intruder.

Charlie began a discussion with Fernando in his native tongue, asking him about his origins and reasons for coming to Texas. Halson abruptly interrupted. The lawmen understood little Spanish, having found it easier to communicate to Mexicans with dollars and pistolas, rather than words.

Juris maintained his composure and moved over to Charlie's motorcycle to assess who he was and what he was after. Amongst the items he found were Charlie's war medals. He could have buried them in the European trenches, but somehow it felt more appropriate to discard them in a more ceremonial manner once he reached Mexico.

Charlie complimented his hosts yet again on their cuisine. Kletman demanded to know Charlie's name and business. He was not going to accept silence or dumb conversation as an answer, and that was exactly what he got.

Kletman let his gun do his talking again. Charlie held firm. The Deputy held his ground. Could there be more madmen in the bush, Kletman thought? Was Charlie working for the few Mexican bandits still alive who dared to make raids into Texas?

One look at Charlie's medals, then his face, told Juris exactly who Charlie was, and what he had done for the last ten years. An accidental injury in 1917 forced Juris to spend the war as a clerk in Galveston Harbor. Each ship that took the doughboys to Europe made Juris wish that he could be joining them. Juris was well informed about the war, and fascinated with its tales of glory. He knew little of its reality.

"These your medals, sir?" Juris asked Charlie.

"Yeah."

"These are real prestigious medals. They're British. And you're not."

"Quite," Charlie responded, in a gesture that simultaneously honored the austerity of the British people and mocked the pomposity of their rulers.

The outcome of this chance meeting was now between Charlie and Juris. Both knew that it would probably lead to one of them not seeing the morning light.

"If you're not British, and you're not a thief, then you must be one man," Juris threatened. Charlie's neck tightened. Juris saw his edge and used it. "Charlie O'Brien...one of the war's biggest heroes," he said with admiration. "Then its most infamous deserter," he continued vengefully.

"It took more courage to leave that war than to stay in," Charlie replied boldly.

Juris saw in Charlie's eyes the courage of a warrior, not the fear of a deserter. It was a look he didn't expect. A more powerful show of force than a whole army of Mexican bandits. Still, there was one question he had to ask. "They were gonna make you a General. Why did you throw all that away?" Juris was confused, even sorrowful.

Charlie remained silent. He didn't understand the irony of his situation either. Charlie and Juris shared a silent moment of reflection, then got back to business.

Charlie took out a fistful of money from the lining of his shirt. It was more than a year's legitimate wages to a skilled laborer, two weeks pay for an equally-skilled thief. To Charlie it was paper. Stolen one way or another, from his publisher or fat-cat bounty hunters who required a lesson in poverty. Some was conscience money, donated by revolutionaries who decided to become economically linked to the system they were ideologically pledged to destroy. Still stolen, and worthless for the life he now wanted. Using it to buy Maria and Fernando's freedom was as good a purpose for it as any.

Of course, there would have to be haggling. With Juris psychologically defeated in the preliminary duel, Charlie had to deal with his seconds, Kletman and Halson.

"How much do you want for the woman?" Charlie asked in a soft voice, eyes fixed on the fire in front of him.

"We don't sell our Mexican cattle to cowards or deserters," Kletman replied. He spit on Charlie's boots, now convinced that the mad ex-veteran was alone.

With plan A gone, it was time to attempt plan B. Charlie got up and walked around the camp, his strides getting longer with each step. He circled the fire, pausing to make a mark in the sand at each of four directions.

Kletman's Winchester and Halson's Colt were a fingertouch away from blowing Charlie's brains into the desert sand. Fernando and Maria closed their eyes, fearing the worst for the Gringo fool.

Halson wet his lips. Kletman smiled like a vulture anticipating innocent prey inside its mouth. Juris said a silent prayer for his fallen hero.

Charlie broke the silence with an old Mexican nursery rhyme. He danced around the fire in a modified Yaqui dance step, bringing in the high-stepping action of a Highland fling, picked up while watching Christmas celebrations in the Scottish trenches. The improvised lyrics were in Spanish, altered to deliver a clear message to the Mexicans. "Reach behind you, slowly. And cut the rope. Grab the guns when I count to THREE."

Charlie's promise was confirmed. Maria and Fernando found behind them a knife to cut themselves loose, and a revolver to use their freedom effectively. They were O'Brien revolvers, built according to his own design with the finest alloys available from Wentworth's factories. What to do with the Texans after their capture would be the Mexicans' problem.

Kletman and Halson laughed at the coward who sung Spanish nursery rhymes and kicked up the dirt with the shuffle of his dancing feet. The source of their self-esteem was always fed by degrading others, and this was an unexpected midnight snack.

Juris was very cautious of this madman who could be so compassionate, but also so deadly. As a lawman, Juris learned to categorize the different brands of craziness in the eyes of dangerous criminals. But Charlie's brand of craziness was very different, not fitting into any category of man born of woman or whore.

As victims close to death, the Mexicans had to expand their perspectives. Somehow they knew that trusting this crazy Gringo was the only way to stay alive.

Charlie shifted into a Metis jig, picked up while union organizing in Manitoba. Kletman and Halson lowered their guns. They laughed at the dancing cigar store Indian with white skin. "The step is easy. Ya just have to let go. One...two...one...two..., one...two," Charlie repeated, like a lunatic drunk with madness.

The lawmen started to lower their guns. Lowering their guard would be next. Two more circles around the campfire, Charlie thought. "You gotta keep going, not stop," Charlie continued, "One...two...one...two."

Charlie was in top form, intellect-wise. But as happened all too often, forces far more powerful than intellect were getting stronger by the second.

Fernando was a man driven by passion, not reason. His anger was too intense to wait for Charlie's signal. He reached into the bush behind him, grabbed the revolver and fired at Halson. It was a clear shot to the groin, delivered to its target by hatred as much as pistolero accuracy.

Kletman aimed his Winchester at Fernando. Charlie ran into Kletman. He grabbed the rifle and hit him with it, breaking the stock and at least three of the deputy's ribs.

Unable to scream with the pain, Kletman fell to the ground. A barrage of gunfire quickly delineated a Mexican and Texan side of a battleground as deadly as any in the Great War. The cottonwood trees were decimated in the first volley. The defenders behind them would certainly be mowed down in the second.

Charlie took cover behind his motorcycle. In one of the secret compartments - the one that was unlocked - an O'Brien revolver model 249. In it were three bullets, all he needed.

Somehow, under the barrage of gunfire, Kletman crawled his way back to cover, taking a badly wounded Halson with him. Using his entry route into the bush, Charlie made out the outlines of the Texans behind the bushes and fired. His shots were deadly accurate, taking out each man with a single shot.

Charlie was much better at shooting bullets than the Mexicans were at ducking them. Maria and Fernando lay dead on the blood-soaked ground, their arms extended out toward each other. Between those lifeless limbs lay one of Charlie's revolvers.

Charlie took the hands of his new, now departed, friends and joined them together. He tried to shed a tear but there were none left. Or maybe there were too many, and if the floodgates opened, the tears would never stop. Charlie was terrified of grief. But he was no stranger to anger.

He took his prize revolver and repeatedly pounded it on a rock, trying to crack its unbreakable tempered steel. "Leave me alone!" he shouted up to the sky, hoping that whoever was keeping him alive and killing those around him would put the curse on somebody else.

For hours, Charlie pounded rocks with unbreakable steel, then, finally, the small comfort afforded by exhaustion. His body craved sleep, but there would be nightmares again. They always came to him on nights like this. Besides, the morning light would bring inquisitive visitors. Death on the open range was far more dignified than in a Texas jail cell, but Charlie still had a strong survivor instinct. A curse or a blessing. Maybe both.

It was time to move on, one more time. South was still the answer, with barely 100 miles of desert left to the border. But the closer you get to paradise, the hotter the flames coming up from hell. There were certain to be more bounty hunters between him and the border. And Charlie had a way of bringing trouble around him, particularly when he was trying to run away from it.

Chapter 3

Charlie's motorcycle was low on gas and badly damaged after the unexpected shoot out at the riverbank. The nearest town was Ralston, Texas. It was barely a spot on the map. It was less than that in reality.

Ralston was once a booming cattletown, nestled at the fork between two rivers. There was always good water, good pasture and good company for all who passed through. Ralston boasted five general stores, three blacksmiths, ten saloons, and an opera house that showcased the best music of Europe, played with a down-home Texas enthusiasm.

But this was 1925. The days of the wild and unfenced prairie ended even in West Texas by 1910. It was now oil that spurred on the imaginations of young men seeking their fortune. Those fortunes would be spent in places like Dallas, Chicago and New York. They would not be made in oil-poor towns like Ralston.

The older men refused to leave, but couldn't come up with any good reasons for the younger ones to stay. Some of them heard that oil would be discovered under the windswept prairie town. Some prayed that it never would be.

Sam Johnson's family settled in Ralston in 1830. His great-grandfather fought for Texan independence from Mexico in 1836. His grandfather fought for independence from Yankee Federalism in the 1860's. The first quarter of the twentieth century found Sam Johnson fighting for his independence against most everyone.

Sam operated a general store and petrol station on the outskirts of town.

The bank held the deed, but Sam kept the Johnson Ranch sign proudly displayed, along with the Lone Star flag, and a Confederate flag that survived ten battles and as many bullet holes. The wood was rotted and the roof barely kept out the rain. The desert was reclaiming the building in a hurry. The road was barely discernible. Ten foot high drifts of sagebrush settled against every wall facing the wind. Desert creatures of all kinds had established homesteads. The crevices protected from the chilling night wind and the hundred and ten degree afternoon sun.

Charlie wheeled his motorcycle into the station and yelled out for assistance. The only response he got was from the wind.

He knocked on the door, gently, so that it would not totally fall off its rusted hinges. The rats squeaked hello and went on their way. He took a few dollars out of his pocket and put it into the mailbox, trying not to disturb a family of spiders which had established residency there.

Charlie helped himself to the gas, then noticed some rusted tools lying around in the dirt next to him. They were just what he needed to repair his bike. Yet another coincidence, perhaps a curse, perhaps a blessing. The two seemed intermingled so much these days. Then, an unannounced visitor from behind.

Sam Johnson was an impressive man in a very unimpressive county. Chaps strapped around his wiry legs, a five-day beard covering his face, and a cantankerous attitude around every word. A double barrel shotgun across his left shoulder, perhaps loaded, perhaps not. "Can I help ya, son?" inquired the crusty old cowboy in a tone inviting courtesy, but demanding respect. He looked barely literate, but could read wanted posters well enough.

Charlie finished filling his gas tank, hiding his face from Sam's inquisitive eyes.

"I left something in the box," Charlie replied. He wasn't looking for any trouble, and conveyed that sentiment as strongly as conversational words allowed.

Sam carefully opened the box and pulled out the money. It was fresh currency, five one-dollar bills. The most the tank would take was a dollar's worth of gas.

Charlie capped his tank, then proceeded to repair the bike in his usual self-absorbed, frantic manner. Sam took a few long Texan strides forward, then noticed the bullet holes which disabled Charlie's two-wheeled steed.

"I knocked," Charlie commented. He could feel Sam's suspicious eyes looking upon him from behind his back.

"Shoulda knocked louder," Sam replied.

"And I waited."

"Shoulda waited longer." Sam spat on the ground. His aim was true, scaring a ground lizard back into its hold.

"I'm not very good at waiting."

"I can see that. Can also see that you ain't goin' nowhere in that."

Sam's prediction was realized instantly. The motorcycle engine broke into pieces and fell to the ground. Charlie yelled out every sacrilegious phrase of discontent in his vocabulary. Sam smiled, gentle laughter in his heart.

"I can fix it," Charlie vowed. In this showdown between man and machine, man would be the one who would walk away alive and victorious if Charlie had anything to say about it. "I can fix anything. That's why they pay me - paid me - the big bucks." Anger became sombre reflection once again.

Sam pulled a 30-30 bullet out of what was left of Charlie's carburetor. "Who shot at ya?" he asked. He spat another wad of saliva at the ground, then waited.

Charlie's neck tensed up. He gazed at a nearby lariat, remembering how they hung anyone who killed Texan lawmen, even if those "peace officers" were the worst kind of outlaws.

Sam continued. "Ya seem like a real desperate man. One who's running' from a real powerful one."

"It's a long story," Charlie replied. His weary mind sensed that Sam's interest was out of curiosity, not greed. Still, Charlie had made many bad decisions when he was tired and disillusioned.

"Seems like yer full of long stories."

Sam put down his gun. "I bet they're real interestin', too. Nothin' too interestin's happened here since they fenced this country in. Built all them superhighways that's taking this country nowhere in a big hurry."

Charlie was touched by Sam's unsaid story and straight-out sentiments. But he was more concerned with survival. Before him lay the pieces of what was the best-built two-wheeled machinery east and west of the Pecos. Sam smiled slightly, keeping whatever jokes that were going through his head to himself.

Charlie eyed a corral of horses behind the general store. "Ya got anything back there that can take me to Mexico? A more honest kind of transportation."

Sam was better at reading a man's tone of voice than understanding his words. Charlie was on the run from the law, all right, but for the right reasons. At least according to Samuel Johnson VI's way of thinking.

The corral behind the store was large, circular, and built with wood fences. Sam would cut off his right arm and both testicles before he would build the square barbed-wire corrals which were coming into popularity in the rest of the West. Inside were animals as wild, independent and gentle as the man whose brand was on them.

Charlie's eye instantly fixed on a fifteen-hand gelding with a large blemish on the outside of his right front cannon bone. Cuts cluttered every surface of the hind-limbs, and his underbelly was covered with hard, leathery scars.

"He's the best three year old I got," Sam commented.

"Five year old," replied Charlie, as he looked at the horse's teeth. "With a bone spur."

Sam smiled that big all-is-fine western grin which Charlie hated when in the west, and yearned for when in the east. "He got in an argument with a fence when he was a colt," Sam commented. "But he worked himself out of it," Sam boasted. "He's a survivor."

"And he's got a kind eye, too." Charlie allowed himself a warm smile, all too rarely felt or seen. "How much?"

"Thirty five. And I'll throw in a saddle and breast plate fer twelve bucks extra," replied Sam.

Charlie peeled out a fresh fifty dollar bill from another lining in his jacket. At last, he saw something he valued, and was grateful beyond measure to buy something that he wanted as much as needed.

Sam stared at the fifty dollar greenback. He had not seen a denomination that high for years, nor a man who had gone so mad with sincerity over a horse that most cattlemen would use for meat rather than transportation. But there was something very wrong here. "You don't wanna haggle?"

Arguing over prices passed time and revived hunting instincts in a once-wild society now ruled by the plow and the slide rule. Sam was puzzled by a stranger who put no value on either money or the pleasures of simple conversation. But, if this loner wanted to throw away his money and pass up the chance to do some friendly economic jousting, it was his loss.

Sam calculated change due back to Charlie with his fingers, losing count three times. "Keep it," Charlie interrupted. He quickly threw the saddle on his new mode of transportation, and friend, then tightened the girth.

Sam pocketed the money, figuring that Charlie had his own reasons for what he was and did, figuring that even if the fresh fifty dollar bill was fake, he could find someone in the next town to given him at least three crumpled ten dollar bills for it.

Charlie loaded his gear onto the saddle. Sam hammered a fresh pair of shoes on the steed. During that brief period of time, young and old outlaw related the pains of their past, and their hopes for the future, with the economy of verbiage and respect for confidentiality so familiar to the Old West, and missing in the new one.

Sam wanted to go with Charlie to Mexico, but his family was being held hostage by bank loans and mortgage payments. He envied Charlie's freedom. Charlie envied Sam's connection to the world of people. But neither one could exchange paths, even if they really wanted to.

After sharing as much camaraderie as he dared, Charlie mounted up. The final farewell handshake was interrupted by a most unusual intrusion.

A flash suddenly blinded Charlie. It was attached to a camera, too broken down to be sellable in Ralston and not old enough to be an antique anywhere else. Charlie instinctively turned his head and pulled his arms in front of his face as quickly as he could, but it wasn't quick enough. "Thank you," Charlie could hear from behind the smoke above the flash. He lowered his arms, not knowing whether to whip his horse into a flat out gallop for the border, or to pull his revolver and shoot it into the camera. A better look at the eyes of the photographer would tell.

Those eyes belonged to John Smith, a fresh-spirited young man trying desperately to become an overly-experienced one as quickly as he could. On his head, a brown fedora with a shiny velvet rim, placed at a slight slant. On his back, a pinstripe suit jacket, a withered cactus flower in its wide lapel. Around his neck, a wide beet-red tie, ordered from the Sears catalogue, secured against the collar of a freshly starched white shirt. On his feet, second hand calf-high boots, holes around the toes and scuff marks on the inseams. Cattleman's boots, customized by at least four hard seasons in the saddle and as many on the ground.

"John. what the hell are you doin?" Sam asked, weary of John's excessive, though well meaning enthusiasm.

"Takin' this man's picture," John replied proudly. He took out a notepad, then fumbled through his pockets to find a pencil that had not been broken or worn down to nothing. "Now I wanna ask him some questions."

Charlie breathed a sigh of relief. This youth was no threat to anyone except, perhaps, himself. But there was something in John that fascinated Charlie. Perhaps it was his intense eagerness to improve himself. Perhaps it was an enthusiasm that had never been dampened or defeated by experience. It would be wise to move on, but it would be more enjoyable to stay a little longer.

Sam introduced John to Charlie, by name, then by family lineage. "Thinks he's the best newspaper man east and west of the Pecos," he added.

"I will be," John countered defensively, as he finally found a three inch whittled down pencil with a blunted tip. He wrote down the date on his notepad, as if it were the first page of a novel that would change the world, and continued. "I got the instincts of a reporter."

"And the dreams of an eight year old," Sam countered. He turned to Charlie. "He does this to every drifter who passes through. Never been more than a hundred miles from here and thinks he knows the world."

John protested, claiming that he had been to Dallas twice, and San Antone at least three times. Sam pointed out that most of those visits took place when John was still in diapers.

Charlie sensed the coming of a confrontation in which he could watch, and might even be asked to participate. It would be fun, and probably harmless.

Deep down, John looked up to Sam. And deep down, Sam respected John's tenacity. But they still enjoyed arguing. There wasn't much else for either of them to do in Ralston, anyway.

John continued to boast about his journalistic instincts with the sureness of a gambler holding a royal flush. Sam called his bluff. “Okay, Mister ‘instinct’. Tell me ‘bout this gentleman here.”

“And if I do, ya’ll buy a subscription to the newspaper I’m starting next week. And it’s not gonna end up in the outhouse this time.”

“And if you lose, then you go back to grindin’ coffee and sweepin’ floors at yer uncle’s feed store.”

“Fair enough.”

John picked up his pencil and walked over to Charlie. His stride was like a cattleman looking at the conformation of a cow at the most public of auctions. “That motorcycle in front. It’s yours, right?” John blurted out suddenly, causing Charlie’s horse to spook.

“Right,” Charlie replied.

“Thought so, thought so.”

John shifted into an even longer stride, accompanied by a hunched back imitative of Sherlock Holmes. “Newspaper work is like detective work,” John seemed to remember from somewhere. “Except that in the news world, *carry on* is guilty.” He then moved closer to Charlie, stopped, and sniffed him from head to toe.

“Ain’t ya gonna ask no questions?” Sam asked.

“Don’t need to,” John replied. “I got instinct.”

Charlie was both touched and amused by John’s ineptness, and touched by his enthusiasm. Sam looked away, embarrassed.

John exclaimed several “okay’s,” a few “it’s elementary’s,” and some new raccooner phrases that were already dated in New York, Chicago, and even Dallas. After an affirmative “bingo,” John boldly announced his findings about the silent stranger. “Born in Waco. Waco, Texas. Born and raised. Will probably die there, too. Married, with four kids. In Waco.”

Sam laughed. John dropped his head in shame, feeling the exit gates of Ralston closing in on him once again.

“Right, Waco, Texas,” Charlie proclaimed with a fake Texas accent. John’s confidence and hope were revived.

Sam stopped laughing. He looked up at Charlie, wondering what his game was. Charlie wanted the privilege of directing the rest of John’s journalism lesson. Sam gave his silent approval.

John continued. “Never seen a big city in yer life, right?”

“Right again,” Charlie replied, with a louder and longer Texas drawl.

John resumed his Sherlock Holmes dance through the tumbleweeds and pressed on, “Never been outside of Texas, and, if you’ll excuse me, never seen the inside of a classroom beyond the fifth grade.”

“You ain’t kiddin,” Charlie said once, then twice.

“Sam intervened. “This has gone far enough. A bet’s a bet.”

“Yeah, but the kid’s got grit,” Charlie interrupted in his natural, cynical tone, and an unmistakable New York accent.

John kicked the dirt in frustration. Sam restrained his laughter, realizing that the contest of wills was fun for him, but had become deadly serious business for John.

Charlie continued. “Sounds like John, here, could get a lot by reading Hemingway. Or Steinbeck. Yeah, Steinbeck. It takes a real man to appreciate Steinbeck.” John turned away from his two teachers. Sam went after him. He’d be willing to go double or nothing with the next drifter who stumbled upon Ralston in his travels.

Charlie gently spurred on his new horse. After a few strides he stopped, then abruptly turned around. He treated himself to the pleasure, and pain, of one more look at the broken pieces of the motorcycle which had been his most faithful companion on this three-thousand mile pilgrimage. “You got a mechanic in this town?” he asked Sam.

“I can fix ANYTHING,” retorted John defensively to Charlie, then to Sam.

“John. That motorcycle in front,” Charlie replied in a tone that was fraternal or paternal, depending on how you listened. “If ya can fix it, it’s yours. It can take you to some interesting places. I hope you can enjoy them.”

Having got the last word in, Charlie rode into the setting sun of the southwestern sky as fast as he could. There were places to go, and important things to do.

“Human” was the best word Charlie could come up with for John. The farmboy-turned-ranchhand didn’t have enough cruelty to make him clever in the eyes of a world growing crueler by the day. John would be eaten alive in New York, Chicago or even Dallas, and not even know that anyone had taken a bite out of his hide.

Better for John to stay in Ralston, Charlie thought. Safer for John AND the world. Eventually they would have to meet each other, with only one winner in the ideological duel. But not today.

Chapter 4

The closer you get to paradise, the hotter the fires of hell, the fiercer the demon's grasp, and more devious the devils become. Such was Charlie's existence, particularly after the fateful deal he made nearly two decades ago with Wentworth.

It was only fifty miles to Mexico now, but the mountains were getting steeper and harder to negotiate. Wentworth's henchmen were everywhere. By 1925, the British aristocrat was a top player in the booming post-war American stock market. He naturally owned the law, and the souls of most of the men who enforced it. At last count there was a price of $50,000 for Charlie's capture, $25,000 for his head. Talk at the bars and cantinas was that there was an additional $100,000 for his testicles, the result of Charlie having followed up on a sexual advance made by Wentworth's daughter, Emma.

Yaqui country was still not in Wentworth's jurisdiction. Like the desert that nurtured them, the Yaqui were unconquerable, even when "successfully" invaded. They had been waging war against the Spaniards and Mexicans for nearly four centuries, beginning with the rebellion of 1609 and culminating recently in the uprising of 1902. Their numbers were down to no more than 25,000 by 1909. Then came the Mexican revolution, which was fought for "land and liberty." The Yaqui shed much blood for this cause, and got no land or liberty in return. Still, they survived on the patches of ancestral land they could take and hold.

The Yaqui were never really conquered on the inside, either. The Jesuits forced the cross upon the Yaqui, but the missionaries were converted very quickly to Yaqui ways. Yaqui "Christianity" had more connections to Mother Earth in the Sonoran desert than to any Holy Father in Rome. Morning prayers had meaning only if they were delivered to the Four Directions, East, South, West, then North.

Adaptability was key to their survival. By necessity, they became the most feared warriors in Mexico. Also by necessity, they became some of the best farmers in North America. Their fields of corn, garbanzos and watermelons yielded bountiful fruit in sunbaked mountains that the Spaniards all too erroneously called desert.

The Yaqui were eager to learn, but not eager to change. The crucifix went hand in hand with the deer dancer and devil chaser at every high holiday. English peas grew side by side with native corn. And practitioners of modern technology were welcomed, as long as they understood that listening was both hard work and a great pleasure, and as long as they were willing to be open to the idea that the mind, body and spirit were inseparable.

Charlie knew how to think with his heart, and had been bold enough to apply that to his study of medicine at Yale University. Western medicine was advancing very rapidly, and Charlie was one of its champion upstarts. He had ten medical research papers to his name by the time he got his degree, all of which were directed at curing diseases deemed "impossible" to treat by mortal hands. On the way he picked up enough credits to obtain a diploma in theoretical physics, a discipline which appeared to enable man to merge with his Creator with intuitive logic, rather than through prayer. The inter-relationship between energy and mass always fascinated Charlie. Transcending to the fourth and fifth dimension was another obsession.

Charlie knew that his destiny lay beyond the university walls. After all, this was part of the deal he made when he was a child, a deal with a man whose voice he could always hear, but whose face he could never recognize. As a youth, an effective life was the same as a glorious one, and even if he did make a wrong turn, well-intended effort would be rewarded. So the rulebook said.

Charlie's efforts in 1906 Mexico were indeed fruitful. He showed the Yaqui medicine men how to open up a man's abdomen and remove foreign objects, tumors, and aneurysms. They showed him how to open up his heart so that life could cure the thousand and two ills that plagued his spirit since birth. Most importantly, there was Diane, a fellow expatriate from Harvard, with whom Charlie could share his medical and spiritual victories. Such was the past.

But this was the present. The view Charlie saw from the high country of Southern Texas was magnificent. The Gulf of California lay to the West. Its breezes could be smelled by an observer with deep nostrils and a complement imagination. To the north lay the snow-capped peaks of the Blood of Christ mountains. They towered over the sun-baked rocks, which boldly showcased shades of red and brown, and which were too magnificent to be given English names.

High vantage points give magnificent perspectives. But they also make one a very visible target. The rest of the journey had to be made by riding low, along the nameless river banks below the mesas and cottonwoods.

Charlie remembered riding these trails in 1911 during the Revolution. He started the war as a doctor, bringing in Yankee medical supplies to Villa's secret camps. Barely a year later, he was the most famous, effective, and uncatchable gunrunner in Villa's army.

The secluded riverbed in 1911 had a rocky bottom, gently-flowing water washing over it at every turn. A team of thirty mules could be taken down the shallow stream without fear of either leaving footprints or hitting quicksand, which can so easily creep up on a rider moving too quickly in these badlands.

But that was 1911.

By 1925, the river had become a dry salt marsh, without trees or water, courtesy of a new dam upstream. A careful rider with 14-hand ponies and knowledge of the terrain would leave tracks a foot deep. If he was in a hurry, he would undoubtedly leave a horse, and probably himself, six feet under the quicksand that had already swallowed up the better half of three cattle herds.

A booming oil town extended for as far the eye could see along the riverbank. White soot settled in the valley below, black smoke hovering above. Day and night, the steel drills rammed into the earth, forcing it to surrender its riches.

There was no way around Paradise, Texas. The high country was teeming with bounty hunters at work, the town saloons overflowing with hired killers at play. Keeping them there was no problem. Wentworth's organization maintained a healthy enough price on Indian and Mexican fugitives to enable a bad bounty hunter to load up with Kentucky whiskey, unload into a Louisiana whore, and still have something to send home to the wife and kids. Still, the big money was on Charlie's hide. Any thinking bounty hunter knew Charlie would have to come through Paradise, one way or another.

By 1925, Charlie had learned to be cautious about good fortune, and to never miss the opportunities it presented. Wind was a constant companion in the desert, except on the day he rode to the city limits of Paradise.

Hot air from the South and cold from the North met in Paradise that day, producing a gray cloud that held in its rain. It also held down the black fog. Charlie rode quietly and quickly, barely a hundred feet below Main Street.

On the other side of Paradise - the high desert. Hot, dry and windblown. Charlie poured a swig of water down his parched throat. He didn't recognize the plateau, and lost contact with the four directions. The sun didn't yet have enough strength to penetrate through the clouds to orient him to the four directions, so he took out his compass. Its needle had faithfully pointed to magnetic north for six thousand miles and nearly two decades. It was stuck. Something that had occurred every now and then, easily fixed by a gentle tap.

Before the adjustment could be made, a voice from behind shook Charlie into another perspective.

"Hold it right there." It was a gruff voice from a man not about to make any compromises. Charlie froze. He heard the bootsteps of a single, very determined man come up behind him. Charlie slowly turned his hand downward so that he would be able to pull the revolver out of his belt in the event that he had to use it. Charlie was so close to Mexico, and he would not stop now. Besides, it was only one man and he was on foot. Maybe it could be settled with a standoff. Maybe not.

The sun broke through the clouds. The man approached closer. Charlie saw a shaft of what looked like a single barrel *45 caliber shotgun* emerging from the intruder's shadow. It was aimed at the sky; maybe its bearer would be slow to use it.

Charlie quickly made his move. He whipped out his revolver and pointed it at the intruder, praying that he would not have to fire, but somehow knowing that he would.

Before Charlie stood a short, wiry man. Sitting above his oversized, fiery eyes - a Stetson hat. It had surrendered its original shape to time and the elements, but still sat firmly around his head. In his belt, a hunting knife worn down from its original size by at least two inches. In his hand, a rusty shovel with a wooden handle.

"Yer on my spot," Clint Milston yelled out to Charlie in a soft tone that left no room for negotiation. Clint was no more than 50, but his sunbaked face would easily put him at 65. His voice was much older. There was barely enough meat on his malnourished bones to feed a coyote.

Clint knew only one way to fight - to the death. There was no way that this rugged individual would give way to such a small thing as a few 45 caliber bullets from Charlie's gun.

Charlie put away his revolver, gave an apologetic smile, and moved aside.

"Thank you," Clint replied courteously. He bowed his head just enough to show respect to Charlie, but not to degrade himself. He retrieved a map and accompanying deed from his back pocket. He laid it on the ground, in preparation to transpose lines on paper to markers in the ground.

Clint walked to the central point, turned to the north, then took ten giant steps. The spot was marked very decisively with a gently prodding of sand with his knife, then a firm insertion of a mesquite branch. He then proceeded ten steps to the west of the center and continued the procedure. Charlie watched, spellbound by something in the old geezer he couldn't put his finger on.

Riding on to Mexico to beat daylight and any roving bands of mercenaries would have been logical. But not getting to know Clint would be a missed opportunity, and a missed opportunity was a cardinal sin to Charlie.

Charlie got off his horse and tethered it to a tree. He pretended to take a sip from his canteen.

"Want some?" Charlie asked.

Clint continued to survey his 300 square foot empire. He looked to the forest of oil wells that cluttered the Eastern horizon and darkened the northern sky and proclaimed, "This land is mine. Paid for it myself. I'll build my own oil city, right here!!!."

He defiantly shook his fist at the oil wells in the distance, then went to the middle of his kingdom and began to dig up the rocky dirt from below the hardened layer of sand above it. His efforts were fueled by the fires of hatred. His pain was given meaning by an open ear from a stranger listening. Charlie didn't know much about the subtleties of casual conversation, but he did know that listening was an active process, rewarded ten-fold. Clint continued.

"Lost the wife to influenza back in 19. Lost the farm to the damn bankers in 22. Had no more than a pocketwatch, twenty dollars, a foundered mule, and a rusty shovel to my name. Coulda traded 'em fer a train ticket to San Antone. Got a brother up there who's got a butcher shop. Said he'd 'take care of me' if times got too hard down here. But the way I figure it, when ya got only two bullets left in yer gun, that's when ya come out shootin'. Ain't no one more dangerous than a man with nothin' to lose. Them bankers and lawyers are gonna find out real quick when I strike oil. On my land."

Charlie peeked at Clint's map and deed. The legalese had fraud written all over it. On the bottom was Clint's signature, an "X" made with the boldest of strokes.

Charlie couldn't tell Clint that his last lifeboat had irreparable legal holes in it. But he felt obligated to say, or do, something. The answer lay in the deepest recesses of Charlie's saddlebags, and were flung in front of Clint in a flash.

"What are these?" Clint asked, looking at one of the handful of Charlie's war medals so rudely dumped in front of him.

"Some extra bullets, to fight the lawyers and the bankers. Golden bullets. I got them off a dead man. He won't be needing them anymore."

Clint squinted his aging eyes, then turned the medals to the western sky so he could make out the images on them more clearly. "They look like they ain't had a good laugh or a good shit their whole lives."

"Quite," Charlie replied. It was the most accurate and humorous description of British Aristocratic stock he had heard in a long time.

"How much you suppose these is worth melted down?" Clint asked.

"A lot more than what they're worth now," Charlie replied. He mounted up, then galloped off. Clint gazed at the medals, trying to make sense of the Latin inscription, even though he could barely read anything in English.

"Good luck, Mister," Clint yelled out. With a single-minded purpose called mad by the meek or complacent, he commenced digging again. "Stop back this way in the spring and I'll buy ya a drink, the best whiskey any where, outta ten dollar drinkin glasses, and cigars...the best, only the best. We'll dance on them oil barons' graves, I tell ya. Dance our goddamn brains out!"

Charlie could hear the old prospector's boasts and promises for two miles. This David had no idea how powerful the industrial Goliaths in the oil towns really were. Maybe that was why this broke but never poor champion of rugged individualism was invisible, and would win the decisive battle.

Energy created cannot be destroyed - a basic rule of physics, Charlie thought. It was a rule he put a lot of faith in, and Charlie was one of the most faithful agnostics east or west of the Pecos.

Chapter 5

"To sleep, perchance to dream" - the line Charlie read on the trail from his leather bound version of Shakespeare's play,s as the light of day and the dark of night became lost in the magnificence of twilight. The pages were worn down by the sweat on Charlie's fingers and the print washed out by overexposure to the elements. But a book such as this on a journey of this dimension was as indispensable as a durable knife or a leak-proof canteen.

It was no coincidence that Charlie's eyes glanced on these lines now. There seemed to be no coincidences in Charlie's life at all, from Charlie's viewpoint. He wanted it that way and life, in retribution, had granted him his wish. The sun had set behind the mountains to the west an hour ago, leaving in its wake a shadowless terrain that could trick the eyes all too easily. Soon it would be dark, making travel all the more difficult.

Charlie was no stranger to trekking long distances under a moonlit sky, but his eyes were growing tired and his mind very weary. Such a man makes mistakes easily, and this was no country in which Charlie could afford to make any mistakes. If falling rocks and lurking quicksand didn't get him, a gunman who had staked out the terrain that afternoon would. Besides, Charlie's horse was tired. The steed had good wind, but was shifting his lead to the left foot too many times for Charlie to feel comfortable about moving on without a rest.

Charlie set up camp in a crevice between two mountains, protected from wind on three sides. The grass was good and would provide his horse a well deserved evening meal. The rocks jutting out of the cliffs, and the thick cottonwood brush alongside of the ravine, would provide him with the illusion of seclusion. Charlie knew that you couldn't hide in the desert, but this place was as good as any. In any case, it had to do.

Charlie hobbled his horse, threw his blanket on the ground, and laid his head upon his saddle. In his left hand was his revolver, loaded and cocked. In his right hand, a Yaqui crucifix, which honored the spirit of Christ and the spirit of the wood from which it was carved.

Charlie listened to the sound of the half-starved coyotes in the distance. Their howls were bold and uninhibited, as if they knew their place in the world and gladly accepted it. He looked up at the endless constellation of stars in the sky and wondered where he fit into the scheme of things.

Nature answered Charlie's question with a bright, flashing comet screeching across the sky, brighter and bolder than anything else, but closer to its death than the spectator stars around it. He could not make out its meaning, but felt that God was talking.

Charlie knew that God spoke to man through the natural world - the huya aniya, as the Yaqui more accurately called it. Within the huya aniya was a spiritual dimension, the yo aniya. This was the inner realm from which the ancients and the honorable ones spoke. From this realm one could feel an intense energy which did not need power to be expressed. It was said to be the strongest in the Bacatete mountains which overlooked the villages in the Yaqui river valley. This vision that could only be named with the Yaqui language was the only thing that had remained untarnished in Charlie's mind over the last decade.

Charlie said goodnight to the stars which gave him hope, then to the land which gave him sanctuary, and closed his eyes. He hoped that dreams would take him to Paradise tonight - or at least provide a solution to his inner illness. Illness is purged from the body by the same route by which it enters. Such was the principle of all ancient schools of medicine. And so it was for Charlie.

He let sleep overtake him and entered the realm of dreams once again. Charlie soon found himself transported to a prison cell a long way from the desert. The cell had steel bars, hard gray walls, and a single toilet that stank from the manure and blood of every prisoner who had ever been held there. From down the hallway came footsteps of armed guards. They had spit-polished black hip boots, blue coats, and shiny badges on their chests. On their hats a latin inscription reading "New York's Finest."

Their leader, Sergeant O'Mally, had a pot belly and a clearly demarcated 5 o'clock shadow on his pale, featureless face. "Mister O'Brien," O'Mally slurred with an Irish brogue that carried the stench of Scotch whiskey. "Ya have a visitor," he continued, with a tone that revealed hatred for Charlie's politics and pleasure at his predicament. Behind O'Mally, three guards holding out their billyclubs, eager to please their master by testing the durability of those sticks upon human flesh and bone.

O'Mally then stood aside and revealed a figure even more imposing, and ultimately far more ugly, than himself. He was wearing a black pinstripe suit and spats. His cufflinks were made of gold, his tieclasp a 14 carat diamond. He approached the cell and let the light hit his face. His face was gaunt, and there was an unmistakable blue tinge around his temples.

"Charlie, you have been quite bad, you know," Wentworth remarked. Charlie was terrified, but he knew that he could not dare reveal it.

Wentworth continued, with a subtext that could only be appreciated by Charlie. "The war is over, and you intend on starting another one. And for what? World enlightenment? You start revolution in the streets. MY streets. MY city. The masses are ignorant and they are happy being ignorant. They just want to be happy. Let them be happy, Charlie. Please."

Charlie responded with defiant silence. Wentworth pulled a neatly folded document out of his breast pocket. "The contract we made years ago. Confess to being in error, and all will be forgiven. We can once again share the reins of power, my Son."

"NOOOO!!!" Charlie yelled out. "I am not your son, and you are NOT my father!!!!."

Wentworth was very good at showing people exactly what he wanted them to see, a talent intrinsic to his nature. With a single glance he showed anger to Charlie and disappointment to Sergeant O'Mally.

Eager to please the hand that kept him in whiskey and women, O'Mally opened the cell door. His men abruptly pushed Charlie up against the walls, securing his arms in an outstretched position - a prelude to a beating which would silence Charlie forever. Charlie feared it, and welcomed it.

"No," commanded Wentworth with a soft tone that overrode the screams of agony reverberating off the prison walls. The guards restrained themselves from unleashing the most vicious of beatings upon Charlie's naked chest.

Wentworth entered the cell and paced around Charlie, eyeing him like a defective piece of meat. The British Aristocrat's gait was relaxed, his stride long. His subordinates stood at attention.

All moral standards they grew up with were replaced by one over-riding desire - to serve the master.

Charlie struggled to get loose from the shackles around his wrist. The harder he pulled, the tighter they gripped. They were another O'Brien-special design, originally intended to clamp arteries that were becoming engorged with blood, adapted for more political purposes.

Charlie screamed as loud as he could to O'Mally, then his men, then anyone else who would listen. "This thing...this monster you call your leader. He kills people. In the worst way possible. He'll kill you too, if you trust him."

O'Mally broke out into laughter. His men joined in, once given permission to display that emotion. "A monster," the respectably-overweight Irish Sergeant bellowed. "A bloody monster. Mister Wentworth, this one's got a healthy imagination alright. Ya want us to give him another beating?"

"No," Wentworth replied. "He'd enjoy it too much." He circled Charlie twice without saying a word. Charlie could imagine the worst. It came.

"Gather those new prisoners. From cell block A, " Wentworth instructed O'Mally.

"But, they're kids, not revolutionary anarchists," O'Mally said. It was his jail before Wentworth bought it, and it was his right to have SOME control in its affairs. "First time offenders, they are. They was the first ones ta throw their hands up in the air when we came in blowin' our whistles."

"And they'll be the first ones to suffer, then die," Wentworth retorted. "Thanks to comrade O'Brien."

Wentworth signaled O'Mally and his goons to move on with a flick of his wrist. The entourage marched down the hallway with a synchronized stride that drove stakes into Charlie's heart with every step. Then, the beating of sticks on bone from adjacent cells, then the cries of pain from youths who were guilty of no more than being naive or idealistic. Flaws to reprimand men, unforgivable transgressions in Wentworth's world.

"You bastard, Wentworth. I WILL kill you. I swear, I will kill you," Charlie screamed as loudly as he could, desperately trying to make himself heard over the cries of torture echoing against the prison walls.

Wentworth calmly took out a cigarette, lit it with his gold lighter, and blew a cloud of smoke in Charlie's direction.

"A deal's a deal. And a gift's a gift," he said by way of commentary. One look in the lighter said it all. The inscription on it still read "Happy Birthday, Charlie," and it reflected an image more clearly than any mirror. One stare into it silenced Charlie into the most painful kind of helplessness.

Wentworth calmly adjusted his tie and cuffs.

"Charlie," he said. "I know who you are. I am the only one who knows who you really are."

"And I'm the only one who knows what you really are," retorted Charlie defiantly.

"Perhaps you do," Wentworth said calmly. "Perhaps you do," he repeated. His understated smile widened and his face took on a paler complexion, revealing a hue more horrible than death itself. He moved down the hallway, whistling "God Save the Queen" as the screams from the adjoining cells grew louder.

Charlie pulled with all his strength to the pain barrier, then beyond it. The shackles came loose. He found himself on the floor, a knife with an ivory handle in front of him. It was well balanced, easily throwable through the bars. Its blade could penetrate at least four inches through Wentworth's back. It was sharp, sturdy and had a crucifix on the handle for look. Nothing could go wrong.. So it did.

Hesitation could be your friend or enemy in combat. It was a matter of timing - and luck. But sometimes it was a matter of conscience. One moment of indecision was all Wentworth needed. Charlie caught a glance of himself in the knife's shiny blade. It was distorted, old, and uglier than anything Charlie could handle. At first it shocked him. Then it blinded him into a dead sleep which could have lasted a month, a year, or a lifetime.

He woke up, knife still in hand, surrounded by heads of the recruits in his New World rebel brigade. They stared at him, praising his name, eyes wide and vague. Charlie allowed the invisible puppeteer above him to make the first move. The sharp blade carved a cross on his chest. Charlie's left hand was then moved behind the right, ensuring that there would be enough thrust behind the blade to penetrate the rib cage at the designated mark. He fell to his knees, on a one way course to the inevitable end he found - and welcomed.

Just then, an echoing voice calling his name.

"Charlie...Charlie."

Charlie felt the pain of a bright light. He looked up and saw a silhouette hovering above him. It moved closer and echoed his name, in a voice from yet another time and place.

Suddenly, the smell of steel and bricks vanished, replaced with the aroma of sizzling bacon and the dryness of the desert morning.

He grabbed his revolver and pointed it at the intruder, but the unidentifiable silhouette kept coming toward him. It squatted down in front of him at point blank range and turned slightly, allowing the light to shine on its face.

It was Emma Wentworth, a very welcomed, yet also very unexpected visitor from a world Charlie had put into his past.

"I made you breakfast," Emma said softly as she laid a plate of bacon, flapjacks, eggs and beans in front of Charlie. He gazed at her in disbelief. She set out some napkins and a blanket, then gently poured freshly squeezed juice into two forty-year-old brandy glasses. From her lips the Communist International theme, sung in the most gentle and playful of voices, even though the words to that Socialist battlecry were originally written to be shouted.

She caught a glimpse of the blood on Charlie's hands and noticed the terror in his eyes. "You having those nightmares again, Charlie? You used to have them every night in New York. Especially after we had really good sex. You never told me what the nightmares were about."

Charlie got up and looked around. He had entered this canyon close to dark. The terrain looked very different in the early morning light. Perhaps his tired mind had overestimated the inaccessibility of this place to bounty hunters. Emma could barely tell the difference between tracks left by a cow, antelope, or jack rabbit. But she found Charlie, arriving in the dead of night in a customized Ford barely a month off the factory floor. The "how's" didn't matter, Emma always had a sixth sense as to where Charlie was, and when he needed her most.

“Where’s my horse?” Charlie asked nervously. He grabbed his rifle and looked up at the cliffs, smelling with his mind’s eye for evidence of an ambush.

“He had these ropes tied around his feet,” Emma told nonchalantly. “I took them off so he could have some room to, ya know, stretch his legs.”

“They’re called HOBBLES. They’re SUPPOSED to prevent him from stretching his legs. He’s probably half way to Canada now!.”

“No he isn’t,” replied Emma in a kind, and understanding tone. She kissed Charlie on the cheek. She pointed down the ravine, to an elegantly spread out banquet of apples and carrots upon which the horse was eagerly dining.

Charlie’s anger at the world was once again quenched by Emma’s lack of it. He laid down his gun and looked at what she had become since he left her in New York barely two months ago.

Emma had taken to wearing trousers, all the time now, her footwear now designed for travel out to rugged places, rather than upward mobility in high-society Long Island. But her hair was still long and golden, and it blew freely in the desert wind. Somehow Emma knew how to maintain the best parts of being a woman.

She also knew what had to be adopted from the masculine persona to achieve true liberation for people of her gender. This was easy. The hard part was deciding who, or what, she belonged to. There were special places in her heart for both her father and for Charlie. She loved both gentle civility and unbridled revolution. She lived each day in the hope that there was room in her heart, and the world, for them both.

Emma was very good at hiding her confusion, and absorbing the pain around her. It was no surprise that Charlie found comfort in her arms, and that she was set ablaze by his defiant spirit. They were both looking for their place in the world, and could rest in each other’s company as long as they were both still drifting.

But Charlie knew that his real place wasn’t in New York or with Emma. Maybe it was the comfort she gave him that made him move on. Maybe it was because Charlie knew that she would suffer for his sins if they stayed together. Fire blazes brightly, but it can also burn flesh all too easily.

That fire blazed particularly brightly in the Spring of 1917, when news of the overthrow of the Russian Czar ignited the world. Russia had been the epitome of feudal imperialism, and the hearts of idealists of almost any political persuasion were excited about the Paradise that could spring from the rich Russian soil that sprouted centuries of human misery. The flower of international brotherhood and a world without war could also bloom. That blossom was to be brief, but the sweet nectar of its flower brought Charlie and Emma together in a wondrous way which neither of them understood. Such was the past.

In 1925, the world was a different place. The dreams that Charlie and Emma shared in New York could not be realized. They would have to adjust themselves to other personal and political realities. But dreams linger on, and can be the most unbreakable of human creations.

Charlie sat down and helped himself to some much needed food. "Ya didn't see anyone following you here, did ya?."

"No. I love you Charlie. I wouldn't do anything to hurt you."

"I know. And if I could, I'd take you to Paradise with me. But it's a long way to Paradise. For both of us."

"I don't understand."

"It's better that way."

"Is there someone else?"

"I don't know," Charlie responded, not knowing himself whether it was the lingering charms of Diane or the deeper wisdom of the Yaqui people which was driving him to renounce the world of his origins. Emma turned away, not knowing whether she should feel hurt, or confounded yet again by the always elusive man whom she loved so much.

Fate intervened again, as it had done so often in Charlie's travels. The forces, or Force, guarding Charlie never let him rest too long in one place. Shots came in from the cliffs above Charlie to the west. Then another volley of bullets from the rocks to the east.

Charlie grabbed Emma and pulled her into a cave. She was too shocked to be scared. Strikes, demonstrations and police reprisals in New York, Chicago and even Appalachia operated according to a set of predictable rules. But shoot-outs in the West were as unpredictable as they were deadly. Nothing like the Hollywood movies, the dime novels, or even Hemingway's masterpieces about the human condition.

Emma held her head under her arms, terrified of the barrage of bullets outside. Charlie gave her a revolver, quickly instructing her regarding its use and relating the necessity of him meeting the assailants out in the open. It went in one terrified ear and out the other, but it was the only explanation he had time for.

A view from the cave entrance was not encouraging. Emma's car was more rubble than car, and all the picnic dishes, pans and pots had been scattered into indistinguishable chips in the desert sand by the unrelenting gunfire. Why the riflemen on the cliffs missed on the first volley, Charlie didn't know. But he knew they would not miss the second time around.

The gunmen's attire was as impressive as their marksmanship. They had bright dusters, dark derbies, and boots that shone brightly in the morning light. These were not bounty hunters who saw Charlie's head as a way to buy two years' worth of cheap women and strong whiskey. These were Pinkertons, highly respectable detectives who owed allegiances to vices more vicious than carnal pleasures. Social prestige is what they sought, a commodity only obtainable in the civilized world by robbing from another. Robbing Charlie of his life here in the Texas desert would enable them to rob many others of their dignity in Boston and Philadelphia.

North of the Rio Grande, there were none smarter in the ways of weaponry than the Pinkertons. But there were none smarter in the ways of the desert than the Texan mustang, a weapon the Pinkertons did not anticipate in Charlie's arsenal. His new horse had managed to hide from the Pinkertons upon their arrival, and was waiting in the ravine.

Charlie grabbed his bridle, scurried down to his horse, and mounted up. He then spurred it on to a flat-out gallop up the ravine, hugging the sides of the cliffs. All Charlie had was a rifle and a horse. But it was his rifle and his horse. Charlie had used fire successfully against the devil's henchmen many times before.

Maby he could pull off this old and familiar trick yet one more time.

Superiority in battle was about position and mobility, Charlie recounted. And, of course, tenacity. The one who is least afraid to die emerges alive, a paradox of war. But whether that axiom held true against fifteen Pinkertons armed to their gold-plated teeth was another question.

Nature was kind to Charlie, providing him with a narrow trail that cut through the valley on the east slope. It was covered with mesquite and cottonwood trees, affording some cover from the downpour of bullets. Charlie and his horse survived the gallop up, but the ammunition pack on his saddlebag didn't.

Fifteen Pinkertons divided by ten bullets was not the kind of arithmetic that made Charlie feel comfortable. He also didn't like how quickly the Pinkertons were advancing on the cave below.

Charlie took aim and killed the one who looked like their leader, straight between the eyes from at least five-hundred yards. His next in command was taken out with a shot through the heart. The rest took cover.

Charlie squatted behind a rock. They knew where he was and, eventually, they would figure out that he was down to eight bullets. A hundred feet below him lay his ammunition bag. It might as well have been a hundred miles away.

Charlie heard an ear-piercing buzz from behind and turned around. Coming closer, faster than any horse on four legs, a cloud of dust. Emerging from it John Smith, riding Charlie's motorcycle.

John seemed to be getting more speed and maneuverability out of that mechanical steed than Charlie ever did. He rode up the back trails of the ravine, as if guided by the dumb luck that preserves saints and fools. Maybe he could hear the gunfire above the engine noise, maybe he couldn't. In any case, it didn't faze the Texan ranch-hand-turned adventurer.

How John got the bike fixed, and found his way to the newspaper story of his young lifetime, Charlie could not figure out. Once again, he wrote it off to something a lot bigger - and perhaps more dangerous - than coincidence.

A stray bullet hit the bike, throwing John off and sending him on a roll which brought him barely twenty feet from Charlie's position. Charlie rushed down to John and helped him up. The Hemingway wannabe was equipped for both a shoot-out and a newspaper story. Combat was a game, not a prelude to tragedy. He pulled out a Colt 38 revolver from under his belt and boasted, "A man out here always has to be prepared."

"Ya got any ammo?" Charlie asked, while ducking bullets from the oncoming Pinkertons.

"Like I said, a man's gotta be prepared," John replied, slowly. He had at least a hundred bullets in his backpack. Only one in five fit a 38 Colt.

"I'll outflank them on the West. You cover me," Charlie commanded John in an authoritative tone at which he was all too good. "Do you know what that means?" he continued in a condescending tone.

"Yep," replied John in a slow drawl. "I take 'em out from up here, and you take 'em out from down there." He loaded the gun, the business end of the pistol aimed at a part of his anatomy which had been used only once in the company of a woman. Charlie pointed the barrel of the gun in a more appropriate direction and calmly explained to John what "cover" meant, hoping that the novice gunfighter would not wind up inadvertently shooting him in the back, or himself in the foot.

Charlie jumped down to his horse below and galloped behind the Pinkertons' flank. He would have to ride *fast enough to not be heard,* but steady enough to get good aim with the few rounds he had left.

Two more bullets found their way into the backs of a team of Pinkertons who had gained position on Emma and were close to doing the same to John.

Armed with an extra Winchester repeater and a fresh belt of rounds, Charlie rode to his next vantage point, prepared to end the career of a swarm of Pinkertons below. Charlie couldn't have asked for a better position. Neither could the lone gunman behind him.

Rand Wilson was a professional of the highest caliber. Since before the first barbed wire was laid out on the open Texan range, he was a lawman who understood the ins and outs of keeping law and order in a country where freedom was the most prized possession.

Wyatt Earp was now doing well as a business man in California. Masterson was making a healthy living as a Sportscaster in Chicago, and Buffalo Bill's Wild West show could still draw in crowds wherever it went.

Rand was a lawman, plain and simple. He was also a dedicated family man, directly responsible for the care of unfortunates cursed with bad health, and misfits who were in heavy financial debt to the Wentworth Empire. The Pinkertons offered Rand a job, a steady wage, and the chance to use his skills in the service of what the former Sheriff could loosely call justice, on a good day.

"Been a long time since the days you were running supplies down to Villa," Rand said, the barrel of his Winchester aimed at Charlie, his finger on the trigger.

"Sorry I made you lose your job," Charlie replied apologetically.

"Woulda lost it anyway. The 'respectable' folks in town wanted me to take care of all their dirty work. Never wanted me at any Sunday socials. Didn't wanna go. Woulda been nice if I was asked."

"What happened, Rand?"

"I got a family. Priorities. Obligations that I didn't bargain for. You know how it is, Charlie."

"Yeah, I do. I think."

"One thing, Charlie. Doing what you have to do isn't always what you wanna do."

"Yeah. I know, Rand."

The talking stopped. Rand lowered his rifle and took three steps back. Then deadly silence. The noise of gunfire below was absorbed by the desert wind. It was one warrior facing another now, in a fight neither of them wanted.

They honored each other with several more seconds of quiet, then said their silent farewells.

"On five then?" Rand said. He turned his back.

"Five." Charlie said, taking his spot, rifle pointed to the ground, his back to the man who had served him as an enemy and a friend.

"Four."

"Three."

On the unspoken count of one, guns were drawn up and fired. The sound of those two shots were loud as artillery, and twice as deadly.

Rand opened his coat. There was a large hole in his chest that no doctor could repair, and his rifle was several hundred feet below. With a smile of admiration - and pity - he looked up. "Sorry, Charlie, you lose. Do you want to finish it, or should I?"

Charlie raised up his rifle and fired another slug, firmly between Rand's eyes. His body fell down the cliff, arms spread out to the sky, Rand's spirit offering itself up to Creator.

Charlie was nicked in the shoulder, but felt deader than the corpse that splattered on to the canyon floor. He fell to his knees, silently begging forgiveness for what he had done, and for what he had to do.

The rules of this local war were clear - shoot to kill. It was the only way to survive, and to protect those assigned to you as friends and allies by the passionless impersonality of fate.

Within minutes, Charlie killed the rest of the Pinkertons nestled in the ravine and the overlying cliffs with deadly accuracy. It seemed effortless, ominously too easy for the bullets to find their marks.

Just as the last deputized bounty hunter fell, six loud shots from the cave below echoed off the canyon walls, followed closely and intensely by dead silence.

Charlie desperately cried out Emma's name, silently offering his soul to any supernatural power who was listening. Still, silence. He cried out again, but the desert answered him with silence once again.

Charlie galloped down to the cave at full speed. At its entrance lay two Pinkertons, freshly killed by 45 caliber shells delivered into the chest and head. One was an older gentleman with a well-trimmed white beard, the other an agent-in-training who had been raising a peachfuzz mustache for the last six months. In the hand of the elder Pinkerton was a note on fine linen stationery:

My Dearest Emma,

In the event that these gentlemen find you, I trust that you will accompany them to the nearest train station and come back to New York.. I have heard that you have been neglecting your studies again. In the event that I cannot meet you at Grand Central, a representative from my New York Company will see that you have all you need to get your life back in order. We will talk about your involvement with Mister O'Brien at a later date, but for now, it is my wish that you return home safely.

Your father,

Sir L. L. Wentworth

Between the lines was a father's love for his daughter, but also the rage of a man who would not accept rejection from those closest to him.

"They said they'd kill me if I didn't go with them," Emma repeated from behind the barrel of Charlie's revolvers, faint irregular breaths passing over her quivering lips.

Charlie gently tried to take the smoking revolver from her hand, but Emma had a deathgrip on its handle. She couldn't take her eyes off the two corpses in front of her. She kept the barrel of the gun pointed at them, fearing that the bodies would give up ghosts that would demand retribution.

First kills are easy to do in the heat of battle, but the why's and wherefore's become lost in the unconscious. Emma would never be sure if killing those two Pinkertons was necessary, but it happened. Maybe the Pinkertons were bluffing. Maybe they were just trying to scare her into what her father thought was a sane decision. In any event, she had crossed the line, and had to deal with it.

Charlie was not skilled in the subtleties of extending compassion in emotional need, but he did have experience in dealing with recruit grief on the battlefield. "You did what you had to do. You saved your own life, and mine," Charlie repeated slowly.

With Emma's blank eyes still on the corpses, Charlie quickly grabbed her wrist with his right hand and embraced her with his left. The gun dropped to the ground. Tears flowed down Emma's face and hot sweat poured out of her arms.

Charlie took Emma outside the cave for a change of air and perspective. He looked up to the big blue sky, hoping for some magic words of explanation that would put things right in Emma's mind and relieve the painful emotions tearing apart her soul.

A cloud covered the sun. A voice echoed from the top of the ravine. "I been shot, I been shot." John was wounded in the shoulder, blood soaking his jacket. The prospect of losing his arm - or his life - drove terror into the budding journalist.

Emma gripped on to Charlie as the blood-drenched stranger came down the ravine. Charlie could get him out of this mess, John thought. It was Charlie, after all, who made it possible for him to leave the deadly comfort of his hometown, and no mentor would ever lead any pupil into a trap from which there was no escape.

A look at his gear gave Charlie even more concern. The fireworks of the morning's skirmish destroyed most of his medical equipment and supplies, ominously leaving his weapons, ammunition and food intact. Amongst the medical goods had been the best drugs, surgical supplies and protective devices that could be bought, borrowed, or stolen North of the Rio Grande. The demolished cargo was supposed to be Charlie's entry visa into the Yaqui community, a peace offering for having walked out on friends and loved ones to fight the Great War in Europe. The supplies would have allowed Charlie to perform his magic tricks with flesh and bone, and ensure that he would be a useful member of the Yaqui community in the event that he wasn't a welcomed one.

But salvage of Charlie's medical equipment and plans would have to wait. John's injury was a familiar one, and it called for emergency measures. The nerves in the brachial plexus seemed to be intact, but the vascular supply was another matter. Loss of blood from even a small bleeder could cost a man out here his life, or at the very least a limb.

Soon after the shotgun was introduced to Northwest Mexico, the Yaqui came up with ways to put together what buckshot could tear apart. Like most Yaqui first aid, the technique required quickness, determination, and a knowledge of the gifts provided by the desert. One of those gifts was brazilwood.

Charlie spotted a tree with the right consistency of bark and gave Emma his hunting knife. "Take this, cut off a branch, and mince it up into small pieces. NOW," he barked, as if still on the battlefield in the Ardenne.

All Emma could do was to mutter half words, then drop the knife into the sand. Charlie rammed it back into her trembling hand, and ordered her to pull herself together, sparing no manner of verbiage to convert her fear into anger.

Charlie settled John onto a soft spot of ground, gave him some brief encouraging words that were more wishful thought than promise, then ran over to the pile of debris that barely half an hour ago was Emma's car. He retrieved a one-inch diameter pipe and scurried back over to John, who was now being held by Emma.

"Smaller pieces. I want smaller pieces," Charlie screamed at her. Emma complied, scared of what might happen to John, and too worn out to have a blow-out argument with Charlie.

Charlie put the wood chips into the pipe. He turned to John. "This is gonna hurt, kid. Hold on to something."

John grabbed hold of Emma's arm. His request for inner strength from her was granted, with an extra helping of compassion. Emma did not know how to care half-way. John was appreciative of that, and appreciation was all Emma really needed to keep her satisfied.

With the first blow of chips into the wound, John screamed, his poise lost. The second was harder, tears of agony streaming down his face. Charlie fired a third blast. The bleeding stopped. John was overwhelmed with pain, his shrieks absorbed by Emma's bosom.

"Now, I think that a more modern approach is indicated," Charlie said. He was detached, carrying himself with a self confidence that bordered very dangerously near arrogance.

Charlie had not used his surgical skills for healing in a long time, but they were as sharp as ever. His hands could work miracles with flesh and bone. It was a claim he attributed to being able to listen to tissue vibration and subtle electric currents with his fingertips. Charlie's speculations on the research laboratory were never wrong, and he seldom lost any patient's life or body part that he deemed savable. With the few surgical instruments still on hand and a few salvageable threats of suture, Charlie was true to form. It was as if he had stolen the sacred books from both God and the devil, and was using them both to cure the world on his own terms.

Emma watched Charlie perform his medical miracles. She had utmost respect for Charlie's abilities, but far more significant feelings towards John. It was John who dared to face a hostile world without the armor of supernatural "talents." He was more concerned with people than populations, and valued heart over mind. Perhaps John would value her for who she really was. Charlie never seemed to, a fact which she finally came to realize.

Charlie spent the rest of the day looking for medicinal ingredients provided by the desert. He would need caliche plants for John's chest pains, rosemary, yerba colarado and alucema for wound dressings, and iodine-concentrating plants as disinfectants.

Charlie also needed to bury the dead, and to write their loved ones about their demise. It was his custom to send a note of condolence, a letter of encouragement, or perhaps some money, to the families of every soldier who died by his side or by his hand in the Great War. Continuing that practice with dead bounty hunters and lawmen was dangerous, but more essential than ever for his psychological survival. Without that, Charlie would be deader than the corpses he buried in make-shift graveyards stretching from the peaks of the New England Berkshires to the West Texas high country.

The high desert provided few branches straight enough to be Christian burial crosses. Still, Charlie provided a Christian burial for Pinkertons who had died doing very unchristian things. Money was something more often stolen than earned in Charlie's eyes. He considered it his duty to collect cash from each dead opponent, and distribute it out of a communal pot to their survivors according to need - as determined by the O'Brien standard.

Agent Billy Thompson was survived by a respectable old Southern family in Memphis and a Creole newlywed in New Orleans. He carried around two wedding photos, maybe in the hope of getting caught one day. Miss Penelope and Bourbon Street Bernadette both deserved an equal share of Billy's reward money, and a lot more.

Agent Bruno Brunkowski spoke barely two words of English when he arrived in Halifax harbor as a stowaway on a Swedish fishing boat. Leaving his mother Russia was hard, leaving a promising political career was even harder. Colonel Brunkowski was one of the most effective Bolshevik commanders in the Ukrainian campaign of 1920. He was also one of its greediest capitalists, and stupidest thieves. Bruno lived a charmed life. The crumpled dollars in his deep pockets and I-owe-you's from gambling on the trail gave testimony to his world-wide reputation as one of the luckiest cheaters on three Continents. Still, there had to be someone in socialist Russia who would miss Bruno and if anyone could find them, it was Charlie's Bolshevik comrades.

The rest were a mixture of professional killers, social misfits, or both. Each got a fair measure of Charlie's attention. There seemed to be nothing unique about them, and Charlie did not relate well to people who weren't unique.

Then there was Rand, his legs and arms extended, his eyes looking up to the Big Texas sky, his grave only two feet deep.

"Goodbye, Rand. Good luck. Hope there's something on the other side of this that was worth all your trouble here." They were the only words Charlie could come up with.

Charlie always dreamed about getting a Viking's funeral. He owed one to Rand. On more than one occasion, Rand could have rode harder, or shot straighter when he was put on Charlie's tail by General Black Jack Pershing's envoys. In return, Charlie robbed supplies for Pancho Villa from towns in Rand's jurisdiction only as a last resort. Rand and Charlie both knew that the arrangement would have to end someday.

One of Emma's half-filled gasoline jugs somehow survived the gunfight. The motorcycle was beyond repair by anyone born of woman, even Charlie, and the Pinkertons were survived by well-conditioned horses. It seemed appropriate to toss gasoline over Rand's body, then set it ablaze with a match. It also seemed appropriate to throw the remaining medals into the inferno.

Also appropriate, the inscription on the grave: "Charlie O'Brien, born 1885? died 1925." The world would know that Charlie was gone. Rand's family would be told where he died, and why. John could write up the story, Charlie thought. Something believable, but still respectable. True to the spirit and, wherever possible, the facts. To Charlie, and Rand, life was about what you leave behind, not what you experience. Rand would get his most important wish. Maybe one day Charlie would get his.

The moon was full, and Charlie was tired, but he couldn't get to sleep. Several times during the night, he caught a glance of John and Emma sharing a fire, then a blanket. Though nothing was carnally consummated, they looked right for each other. Charlie saw Emma cuddle up on many cold nights and mornings in their loft at Bleeker Street, but her smile was never more contented than under the cold Texan desert sky. John looked like a real man and perhaps for the first time in his life he felt like one.

Charlie left a note on the Pinkerton bedrolls they used as a pillow. " I wish you both much joy, and as much happiness as can be afforded people who are really alive. You both deserve such a gift, and birthright."

By sun-up, Charlie was well on his way to Mexico. By noon, John and Emma would be on their way to places and experiences not yet dreamed of in their hearts or minds. It was painful for Charlie to know, but the way things were supposed to be.

Freedom brings pain, all too often on life's terms. Charlie would never be the exclusive recipient of Emma's special warmth. He felt alone, even scared. It was ironic punishment for taking Emma for granted for so many years. But it was a price he had to pay for what he hoped would be a greater reward somewhere in the Yaqui River Valley.

Chapter 6

Finally, the Rio Grande. The river was shallow and muddy, barely a creek. But to Charlie's wishful eyes, it was a clear mountain stream overflowing with water that could cleanse the evil out of even the most corrupted souls. He wasn't the first to give a mystical significance to this very common river.

The stream of slowly moving muck separated two cultures for as long as anyone could remember. The terrain looked the same North and South of the Rio Grande, but the feeling you had when you rode over it was always different. No Texan would even dream that the Lone Star state would extend its political boundaries South of the river, and no self-respecting Mexican would ever allow it.

Charlie dismounted and gave a silent prayer, delivered on his feet. He could hear the quiet here louder than anywhere else in the desert.

Contentment found little breathing room in Charlie, and his mind again slipped into worry. He had heard more than his share of stories from lone, drunk veterans who couldn't find their way home after three years of war. He was away for at least ten.

But there was no time for reflection, and less for self-pity. Wentworth's reward was payable in pesos or Yankee greenbacks, and well-seasoned bounty hunters knew how to avoid, or negotiate, with lawmen on both sides of the border. Only the Bacatete mountains would protect Charlie, and they were still at least three days ride to the south.

It was only early fall, but the landscape was already revealing its many personalities with a constellation of colors. They excited Charlie's eye, and somehow provided signposts for his journey, a sojourn that would involve many miles under the hot sun, and intensive internal surgery on his diseased soul by physicians he could feel but not see.

But pain was for later, a victory celebration was in order now. Charlie hand-galloped across with a yelp loud enough to be heard for at least twenty miles, but he didn't care who was listening. This scream was one of joy, not defiance. Finally, Charlie felt free of both Wentworth and the hatred he harbored for the industrial monarch.

Renewed by the muddy waters, Charlie moved on in an effortless lope that seemed to last for at least ten miles. The ties to the old world of death were gone, connections to the new ones of life were beginning. It was the nature of leaving one stage of life and moving on to another.

Building a new life was something else, and presented a difficult task to a man like Charlie. Life is a cycle of trios, involving creation, maintenance and destruction. Young idealists like John and Emma were very good builders. Most everyone else worked as hard as they could at maintaining the status quo.

Charlie was a natural destroyer of systems gone bad, of those that had outlived their purposes. He fit his niche all too well. Life without fighting Machiavellian monsters like Wentworth was something new. And frightening.

The desert heat came early that morning, and even Charlie's horse could not keep running forever. He was facing the world naked, perhaps for the first time.

A man who cuts ties with the past, and who comes into nature's domain, has to operate according to the rules of God, not those of man. And one of the most important of God's rules is that there are no rules.

The horizon seemed infinite. Charlie found himself overwhelmed by its bigness. He rode for several more hours, but they seemed like days. The mountains became higher and the ground rockier, until it seemed that he was riding on top of the bare skeleton of the earth itself.

Time and space had no meaning here. The events of the previous day seemed like lifetimes ago. The memories of ten and even twenty years ago could be touched with one's hands. Past, present, and future were melded into one entity which could be felt by the spirit, but not defined by the mind.

The spiritual and material were the same in this world. An illusion or a mirage out here was as real as any hard fact anywhere else. Even depth perception seemed to be lost. Rocks, mountains, trees and forests were both far and near at the same time. Einstein was right; time is relative, and a measure of man's experience. But Einstein was not here to give Charlie a lesson in physics or spirituality. Or was he?

Indeed this felt like the huya aniya, the place where spirit and matter are intermingled. It was this place, this condition, which gave the Yaqui their strength and wisdom. And it was the huya aniya which protected even Christ himself from the forces of evil. The Yaqui valued both Jesus and the huya aniya and needed them both. Charlie did, too.

Knowledge was easy for a man such as Charlie. Wisdom was something else entirely. Charlie was willing, and willingness is all that either Jesus or the huya aniya demanded.

The hours dragged into chilling nights and boiling hot days. Charlie and his saddle horse became comrades very quickly. Their bond was based on an understanding which could never be expressed in words. Charlie thought about giving a name to this animal which had been so loyal in service and independent in spirit, but he could not. Even if he did, the name would probably be as unsuitable as the one which the horse had picked for Charlie. They were stuck with each other and were both lost, each hoping that the other would know the way. Somehow, the arrangement worked.

Not the same could be said of Charlie's compass. The needle had faithfully pointed to magnetic North for ten years. Charlie could always smell his way to where he was going if he knew where North was, and he always knew how the land fit into the Four Directions.

The closer he got to the Bacatete high country, the more the needle jiggled, then spun around with a mind of its own. The sun ducked in and out of the clouds, denying Charlie of its location or any shadows he could use for direction. The mountains didn't help either, proving at every turn that the shortest distance between two points was a circle.

Water was as scarce as perspective. It was enough to keep the horses going, but barely enough to keep Charlie alive. No wonder there were no animals here. At least none that would show themselves.

Charlie's horse was startled by a rabbit popping out of a small tunnel on the side of a slate foothill. The horse spooked. Charlie's legs still had some brains left in them. He survived a violent rearing and dead out run on top of the saddle. His food rations didn't do so well, plummeting down a deep canyon.

The jackrabbit stood proudly on its rear legs. Fate provided Charlie with the coincidental loss of salted rations here, and maybe with the gain of fresh rabbit. He took aim with his rifle, cocked the hammer, but couldn't fire.

The foot-high jackrabbit stood taller than any human giant in Charlie's experience or any mythology. This was no ordinary jackrabbit, Charlie thought. His blurry eyes confirmed it. The hare took on the shape of a man, his face unrecognizable but still familiar. It could have been the old curandero's face, or it could have been another one of the many illusions the desert has in store for visitors with active imaginations and desperate spirits.

"Which way home? Which way home?" Charlie asked. If this rabbit-spirit was as smart as he looked, he would know what Charlie wanted, and why.

Silence again, the quiet of the desert louder than ever. "Which way home? Which way home?" Charlie screamed. He was through being whispered to by the Spirits, and demanded a straight answer.

He reached out to the ghost in front of him, grabbing him by the shoulders. Between his clenched fists was thin air, then inside his mouth, desert dust. Up ahead was the rabbit running up a steep ravine.

Charlie's geographical sense told him that the rabbit's path up would be the hardest way over the pass, or a dead-end trail to a box canyon. So did logic. But geographical sense had worked against him ever since he rode into the Bacatetes. Charlie respected the rules to be different in these mountains, but not to be upside-down, inside-out, and altogether missing - all at the same time.

At each turn, the rabbit darted in and out of view, leading Charlie into terrain filled with brush, stones or deep sand. The only way Charlie could survive was to trust the floppy-eared guide - so he hoped.

The air got thinner. Soon, all connections between mind and body were lost. Charlie watched himself run, walk and then crawl up terrain that looked more like the dark side of the moon than anything on earth. His feet bled, and his fingernails were scraped down to the quick.

"Keep on fighting till you forget what you're fighting for. That's the only way you win.." They were the only words that surfaced from his half-mad, half-dead mind to his sunbaked lips. Again and again he said those immortal words which proved to be so true, both in war and peace.

Still, the rabbit kept up the pace. The horses, desert animals that they were, followed with little trouble. Charlie pressed on, each step digging deep into the now empty reserves of physical stamina. Was this trek a pilgrimage to heaven or a death march to hell? It had to end somewhere - maybe.

Then, the breaking point. Not even the spirits could take a man through nine pain barriers. Charlie collapsed. The ground felt hard. But the prospect of dying in limbo harder. One more step, so he could die on his feet.

One step was all he needed. He opened his eyes. Then - a mirage. But one which was too magnificent not to be real.

The sight of the Bacatete range below felt like a view of the ancient Greek world from the peak of Mount Olympus. Suddenly, he felt embraced by the bigness of his surroundings, not overwhelmed by it. The superman of science, who was so good at predicting the patterns of matter, welcomed the unpredictability of infinity. The "big lonesome" - finally.

The rabbit popped up again, then disappeared into a hole. Charlie still did not know his way, but he did know the direction he had to take - forward.

That direction led to a badger, then a coyote, then a group of gophers. They helped connect him to the Four Directions again, then to geography.

Soon, other messengers from the huya aniya came to speak with him. There were deer, wild hogs, birds and snakes. All had things to say, and Charlie had learned the importance of being a good listener. Times were good, and the freedom-seeking loner felt connected.

He rode the high country on his way to the Yaqui river valley, aloof and on his own time. It was a longer route to take, but the view was well worth the extra time and trouble.

There was a special vantage point he had always liked. To the west lay a clear view of the ocean, the Pacific breezes having a special quality to them that high up. Mountains to the North, desert Badlands to the East. To the South, people who brought it all together.

Two Yaqui hunting parties met in the foothills below, one coming in with a small mule deer, the other with tales about a bigger one that got away. They greeted each other in typical Yaqui manner. A man touched himself on the left shoulder, then his comrade on the left shoulder, then grasped his friend's hand in a backward movement. When done with rapid and enthusiastic motions, it seemed like a dance for life and a celebration of victory.

It was fitting that this victory-dance was done every day. Every day a Yaqui stayed alive was a victory, and every other Yaqui was the closest of teammates. 1925 presented particular threats from opposing teams.

The rocks were witness to the beginning of the troubles. By 1650, the conquistadors had forced the Yaqui to become Christians at the point of a sword. In retribution, the Yaqui convinced the Jesuit missionaries that the huya aniya was just as important as Jesus, resulting in a faith that was both Yaqui and Christian. The Yaqui then used the spiritual strength from that faith against the Spaniards in ways they could understand. Yaqui spears and arrows forced many bold Spaniards into a hasty retreat back to Mexico City or Madrid. Yaqui tenacity and honor intimidated some of the most ruthless conquistadors into alternative careers as Franciscan monks.

The century-old cottonwoods saw a completely different type of invasion. Not to be outdone by the Yanks, the new Republic of Mexico was fueled by dreams of wealth, power and expansionism. By 1820, the Yaqui wars started again, the blood of some vicious, and a lot more innocent, people staining the Sonoran desert bright red. Guns and bayonets ended the lives of many Yaqui warriors. But it was the dispersals that nearly destroyed the Yaqui people.

It started small. Yaqui unlucky enough to be captured in battle were sent to work at the haciendas in the Yucatan or the silver mines on the Pacific coast. Then, the object of Federale invasion was to kidnap people, rather than claim land. Men were given the opportunity to be employed by the haciendas. Women and children were rescued from their "savage" lives in the wilderness. Biting the hand that enslaved, then fed, you was not only bad manners, but dangerous to one's health. Attempts to escape back to the Yaqui homeland were punishable by death, or worse.

Then the seductions came. By 1900, barely one in twenty Yaqui still in the valley bearing their name was literate in Spanish. Those who could read the language of the Federales were often very quick to become conversant in the ways of law and military power. Those who chose to remain illiterate could read the minds of the Mexican schoolteachers and their armed escorts all too clearly. In the battle between the assimilation-driven "mansos" Yaqui and the rebellious "broncos," the Federales always emerged as the winner.

By 1909, most of the Yaqui had been killed, were held captive on the haciendas, or had been assimilated into Mexican society, courtesy of President Diaz's military and dispersal program. Then, in 1910 - retribution.

Diaz had stolen what he could from Mexicans and Indians alike. Revolution was in the air, and the Yaqui were up for grabs to the most honorable bidder. The most successful was Mayturena, a Sonoran aristocrat who had found it more rewarding to be kind than cruel. Most Yaqui believed his sincerity. Some didn't.

The Yaqui quickly earned the reputation as the fiercest and most effective in the Revolutionary forces, particularly when they disobeyed their European-trained commanding officers. Every Mexican Revolutionary General wanted as many bronco and mansos Yaqui as he could get, and promised them whatever he could to ensure their services.

Diaz's removal from office pleased a battle-weary Mayturena. The prospect of a civil war to decide who would sit in the Presidential Palace didn't. After the assassination of provisional President Madera, Mayturena handed over his political assets to Obregon, including his Yaqui.

Mayturena's Yaqui gave valiant service to General Obregon in his struggle for power against Zapata, Villa and so many others.

Bronco and mansos factions were both after "land and liberty" pledged to them. Obregon quickly rose to the top, then selectively down-sized his army. His termination of employment notice to the Yaqui took the form of an army, with orders to remove them from their homeland in 1915.

Sixty Yaqui warriors died in the defense of the Bacatetes and the eight towns on the Western slopes. The scheduled wave of Mexican colonization of Yaqui land did not take place. Obregon moved on to finish his political business in Mexico City with egg on his face.

By 1920, Obregon had become President, with a mandate to bring Mexico into the 20th century. It was to be a centralized, industrialized society, competitive with England, France, and even the United States. A new society, with new agendas, unhampered by promises made to old allies such as Pancho Villa or the Yaqui.

By 1922, Obregon made his assault on Villa. By 1925, he was mounting an attack against the Yaqui. The ten-year "truce" had been isolating, and no one could hold back the lava from bursting out of the volcano. Who would win was an issue of wills. That innocent people would get hurt was a matter of fact.

Charlie's vantage point from the high country of the Bacatetes said it all. To his right, the hunting party, a drummer and flute player joyfully improvising on a familiar Yaqui theme as a prelude to a well-deserved meal of beans and deermeat. To his left, a Federale train, speeding down a newly-built set of sun-baked tracks, each cargo car sealed shut and protected by at least ten Federale soldiers carrying German manufactured long rifles.

Charlie wasn't sure if the rifles were O'Brien models or not, but that was immaterial now. In the Texas cantinas, Charlie's ear caught a few half-stories about a revival of the dispersals. True, the narrators were using second hand information embellished by tequila and a gullible listener. Maybe the heavily guarded trains on the sand-flats were carrying gold and silver to Mexico City. Or maybe they were carrying away human cargo. The outside world would never know, and neither would Charlie.

His days as a revolutionary were over. He had no desire to destroy a people by trying to liberate them. Besides, the mountains had protected the Yaqui and the Mexicans from each other, and those peaks had more authority here than any legal document. Little did Charlie know that the bucolic Yaqui river valley he was riding into would be the site for the most decisive battle of his life, with far more at stake than he could ever imagine.

Chapter 6

Charlie finally reached the mountains overlooking the village of Vicom. The anticipation of coming home for the first time in his life energized his tired spirit.

He had avoided contact with Yaqui, sticking to the high country. Whether it was because of his rustiness in their language, or because of his shame for where he had been and what he had done, he was not sure. But one thing was certain, Charlie had to see Diane.

Over the years, he had heard stories about an English-trained Yaqui woman doctor in this area. But the stories were old and were not being told too much anymore. Maybe Diane had moved on. Maybe she stopped being English.

Before the welcomed and dreaded meeting, Charlie had to prepare himself. When farewells were said in 1914, the wrong things were said and the right things weren't. A decade let the true feelings between them get distorted by lingering resentments and desperate hopes.

Diane knew what made Charlie tick more than any woman alive, and he knew it. He kept writing, but got no responses. Maybe she tried to write to him, too. He probably wouldn't have answered.

Charlie hoped that a well-chosen sentimental gift would make her feel less hostile about his unannounced return. He needed some kind of shield he could hide behind once the emotional daggers started to fly. For all his physical courage, Charlie's heart could be easily pierced and did not heal well.

The architecture of Vicom had changed little since the Diaz dispersals. The Mexican colonists attempted to upgrade the three-hundred-year-old Yaqui town, but the desert would not allow it.

But the twentieth century did establish a foothold in Vicom. A general store featured the finest of goods, displayed through one of the only glass windows in town.

In back of the store was a mechanized ditch digger, the first of its kind to be introduced to Yaqui country. Yaqui farming was often more efficient than any Mexican operation, but it was far less productive. This method of irrigation would give the Yaqui more money and more leisure time, Charlie thought.

But the only thing the machine was providing was a home for spiders and shade for the lizards. All that was needed was petrol and some repairs. Charlie's pocket change could put enough gasoline to keep it going for a year and he could fix anything, mechanically-speaking. A trick to pull out of his magic ten-gallon hat for later, he thought. But, first things first.

Inside the store was a variety of dresses, scarves and jewelry, tastefully selected and displayed with pride. Behind the counter, his back turned to Charlie, a Yaqui gentleman in a three piece suit and spit-shined cavalry boots, assessing inventory from the top of a homemade bamboo ladder.

Charlie found himself roaming toward a bright red dress with gold trim on the hem and around the shoulder blades, a matching silk scarf. There was no price tag on it, but it had to be the most expensive item in the store. Elegance and flare seldom came cheap when in the same package. Then again, most of Charlie' money was "stolen" from Wentworth's banks, and from publishers who had overpaid Charlie for his writings when revolution was fashionable. Spending it on Diane seemed like the right thing to do, somehow.

"This one," Charlie commanded in Yaqui, with poor grammar and worse diction. He moved on to the jewelry collection.

Charlie assumed the clerk was listening, and that he was a mansos. Mansos Yaqui knew that subservience was the way up the assimilation ladder, and this mansoso was very proud of the second-class station he held in a fourth-class village.

Charlie continued in Spanish, "I came down here with a special woman years ago." He picked up an elaborate turquoise and silver necklace that transformed the sunlight coming in from the window into sparkles that nearly blinded the eye. Reminded of the good times with Diane, he lapsed into English.

"I have to convince her that I left for the right reasons. And that I came back for the right reasons, too." He paused, handed the clerk the necklace, and boldly continued in Yaqui, "I'll take these."

He moved on, picking the most decadent-looking accessories he could find. Shoes. Hats. Bags. Jewelry. It would be a festive reunion, Charlie thought. A royal wedding of dignity - soul mates.

The clerk had other plans. Charlie turned around and noticed that the predictably subservient mansos replaced the elegantly-styled items Charlie had selected with the simplest garb in the store. The gift box was a bamboo crate. The bow, a stem of sage brush, more twig than flower. Charlie immediately protested, indignant and loud, first in English then in Yaqui.

The clerk smiled and calmly interrupted, in English. "Diane's tastes have become very simple. And she still holds a warm place in her heart for you, Charlie."

Charlie struggled to recognize the voice and the face. The mansos' smile widened.

"Jose Fernandez? Is that you?" Charlie said, with a cheerful camaraderie he had not experienced for a long time.

Jose gave Charlie the traditional Yaqui greeting, commencing with a touch on his left shoulder. Charlie was rusty with the movements, but kept up with the action. The salutation culminated in a laugh shared by both parties, as they eyed each other once again.

"Is that you underneath that tailored suit?" Charlie asked.

"Is that you under all those wrinkles?"

"I came down here to find out."

"Welcome home, Charlie."

It took a lifetime, but Charlie finally earned the right to have those three magic words spoken to him by someone who meant it.

Jose and Charlie talked about good times and bad times with a fond remembrance for both. Not talked about was the revolution.

Jose's intelligence in military matters made him a Colonel in the 1910 Mexican Revolutionary forces. His lack of insight in politics made him pledge alliance to Obregon without a second thought. Obregon's 1915 invasion of the Yaqui valley broke Jose's heart as well as his spirit. Still, he never stopped believing in the system, knowing fully well that Obregon was in charge of it and would be for a long, long time. But even though Jose had a Mexican mind, he still had a Yaqui heart.

The reunion was warm, but brief, and rudely interrupted by a man in three-point sandals and white trousers. Strapped to his shoulder, a Winchester 30-30. Under his belt, a large machete and two Colt 45 pistols, loaded and cocked. "Welcome back, Charlie," he said. The words drove terror into the Gringo pilgrim's heart.

Diego Garcia was a bronco Yaqui who was the most dangerous kind of warrior, in war or peace. He hated life and welcomed death, every waking thought channeled into one purpose, which was to destroy the Republic of Mexico. He calmly helped himself to anything in the store that could be used toward that end, beginning with the selection of machetes Jose laid out as farm implements.

"The REAL Yaqui need a man like you," Diego said, eyeing the weaponry Charlie was still carrying around with him, and remembering how skillfully he had used it.

Charlie remained quiet, his voice held hostage by shock. Jose's silence was held down by a volcano of anger. Diego continued, enjoying the control he had over his former Revolutionary comrades.

"Charlie, did you hear that Villa was killed? Assassinated."

"Yeah. I did," Charlie replied.

"Without him, Diaz would still be President. Rumor here is that Obregon had him assassinated. Did you hear that, Charlie?"

"Yeah. I did."

"I never trusted Villa. He hired too many Gringos. I always got the feeling he was using us. I suppose he was using you Gringos, too."

Charlie answered with a very heavy silence. Diego knew how to find out what troubled a man most and how to use it against him. Diego wasn't sure about Charlie's alliance in the personal war he had going with the Federales. But he was sure about where Jose stood, and prepared his psychological attack appropriately.

Diego moved to the gun and ammo rack, helping himself to the "hunting" equipment with a sadistic smile.

"Charlie. I think you've heard that the dispersals are starting again. Just rumors."

"Yeah. Just rumors."

"Of course, we can negotiate with President Obregon. Some of us still think that he can be trusted."

Jose turned deep red, his fists clenched. Charlie felt compelled to interrupt.

"Talking's better than fighting, Diego."

"Maybe. Maybe not," Diego continued. "Maybe some of us don't care about land. Maybe some of us don't care about liberty. Maybe some of us don't care if our children get carted off to the new haciendas in the Yucatan, Mexico City, or..."

Diego's words were stopped by Jose's hand, choking his neck. Against his throat, Jose's Bowie knife, its blade having not been used against human flesh for a decade. It was Jose's time to talk.

"My mother and father both died in the haciendas. I fought with Mayterena as hard as you did. But I was more concerned with saving our people than killing the Federales. We can't win your way. They'll kill us all, Diego, every one of us this time."

Charlie could not make out all the Yaqui words, but the meaning was clear enough. It was time for him to leave. Jose and Diego had to settle their stand-off in their own way. He approached the two Yaqui warriors while they were battling each other with their eyes and calmly asked Jose how much money he owed for Diane's gifts.

Jose's hatred for Diaz and Obregon overcame his resentment for Diego. He lowered the blade and put it back in its sheath. "I can't take your money, Charlie."

"How much for the dress, the scarf and necklace? You have a family to support," Charlie continued, as he pulled out a fistful of money.

"Two hundred," Diego replied.

Charlie put the money on the counter, fully knowing that the bullets would find their way into Federale soldiers very soon in Diego's private revolution..

"And eight hundred more for the ammunition and the guns," Diego continued.

Charlie put a fistful of pesos and greenbacks on the counter. Diego offered him a Yaqui greeting in return. Charlie accepted it, but he did not execute his motions with any joy or levity.

Charlie and Jose agonized over the soundness of the decision to allow the renegade Yaqui warrior to have his way.

Diego gathered his belongings, the ones he brought in and acquired. “You still got Gringo guilt in you, Charlie. We can use that,” With that, he left.

Charlie turned to Jose. “Are there any other surprises I should know about?” There was no way Charlie could prepare himself for the answer.

Chapter 7

Charlie's journey took him back up to the Bacatete high country. Jose led the way up the steep ravines and onto thickly-wooded mountain trails barely wide enough for a jackrabbit. Charlie knew where he was being led, but could never have found his way by himself, even though his compass needle was back to obeying the laws of physics, rather than the wishes of the Spirits.

The destination was a small mountain village embraced by a rim of thick willow and cottonwood forest. The community was undetectable from the air. The best Federale cavalry scouts could ride past it without noticing its existence.

A small clearing on top of the overlooking ridge gave Charlie a clear view of a village which every Yaqui knew, but which bore no Mexican or Gringo name. This place served well as a shelter for Yaqui hiding from Federale troops. From it, adults could wage war and their children could enjoy peace, a necessary legacy to pass on to the next generation to guard the Bacatetes.

The buildings of the village were made from bamboo, mesquite and cottonwood, according to Yaqui tradition. But there were nuances on that timeless theme which were uniquely Charlie's, incorporated sometime during his long absence.

To Charlie, patience was a vice, not a virtue. He could never accept things as they were - even when they worked. Especially when they worked. In his obsession to do one better than God, Nature and the Yaqui, designs sprang out of his chronically-restless mind which would maximize ventilation in the boiling hot summer, keep out the autumn rains, and keep the cool winter night outside.

The Yaqui were traditionally a selective people, taking from the outside world only what they needed to keep their bodies healthy and their spirits alive. On some matters, ten years ago they complied with the recommendation of the over enthusiastic Gringo wannabe. On other matters they knew better. But they always listened, a skill Charlie learned slowly, with the help of Diane, his Yaqui almost-wife, whose soul somehow survived the Victorian oppression of an English hacienda during childhood, and the sterility of an Ivy League medical education in the prime of her adult life.

One look at the building in the middle of the village confirmed the rumors about the English-trained healer who incorporated the wisdom of the curanderos and the cleverness of twentieth century biomedical science. Bought, borrowed, and stolen hospital supplies were visible through the open-aired windows. But vent and roofing "O'Brien" improvements made on the adjacent dwellings were noticeably missing, dismantled after Charlie's hasty departure. The climate had extracted their revenge on the building for the better part of a decade.

Maybe Diane held out against architectural reason to give him a gentle ribbing upon his return, Charlie thought. As he looked down over the village from the back of his well-muscled sixteen-hand high Texan quarterhorse, he knew in the bottom of his churning gut that Diane had ten years to sharpen the hatchet, and had no intentions of burying it without some damn good explanations.

1914 was not a peaceful year, politically or emotionally. During the blow up between Charlie and Diane that woke up the entire Yaqui valley, all the wrong things were said, and none of the right things were. But there was more at stake than an unsettled love affair between two people who never stopped caring about each other, and who were still capable of doing each other irreparable harm.

Jose brought Charlie's attention to a field where Yaqui children were playing soccer with a deerskin ball. Both sides made excellent progress in moving the ball, but no one thought of keeping score. Joviality was shared equally by all except one player, who laughed a shade less enthusiastically than the others, but who maneuvered the deerskin ball over the hollers and brush with far more agility. His skin was pale brown, and there was a special fire in his bright blue eyes.

"His name is Carlos," Jose commented. He refrained from saying any more, feeling that it was not his place. Jose had a natural instinct for knowing when to interfere in people's private affairs, and when to step aside.

"He's got his mother's love for life. And none of my hate for it," Charlie commented to Jose with a warm smile.

Charlie always wanted a son, but he secretly feared that the legacy holding his own soul hostage might be passed down. It was a relief to find his biological offspring so full of vitality, and seemingly immune from his own obsession with death.

"Diane wanted you to know, at first," Jose said. "Then, she changed her mind."

"Why?" Charlie asked, open to any answer, no matter how painful.

"That, you will have to ask her yourself," Jose replied sternly. It was a tone Jose used only on the most serious occasions, and not one he liked to use.

Charlie's breath was stuck in his throat, his tongue held hostage by fear. As a member of the warrior cult, he feared no enemy on the battlefield, but matters of the heart were something else entirely. His fear was escalated to terror as Jose turned his horse around and spurred it on at a brisk hand gallop back to town. Charlie was left alone overlooking the village, naked between two worlds. A glance at Diane through the hospital window made the warm, gentle Southwestern breezes feel cold and bitter.

A "no" from her now could destroy his life. Terror turned into indecision, and Charlie felt himself glued to the saddle on the overlook. That indecision was certain death for any soldier in battle, and was even deadlier in peacetime. The horse would indulge Charlie's catatonic stare, but the desert and the Yaqui would not.

Charlie listened as hard as he could, trying to connect to the center of himself - to hear the mantra. He breathed deeply, closed his eyes, and prayed. He didn't even know he was praying, but he was answered anyway.

Down below, an Elder began a story to an audience of children, then adults. The old man spoke with the same voice to all, the internal message received differently by each listener.

Charlie snuck up closer so he could hear the words. Though not conversant in Yaqui, he recognized the story instantly. It was the story of Yomumli and the little Surem people. It began before the time of the Spanish conquest, when the Yaqui valley was known as Sure, after its people, the Surems. The Surems were children of Yomimily, the mother who created all the Indians.

The land of Sure at that time did not have any farms, the wilderness providing enough plants for the people to eat. The animals roamed the earth and waters freely, and never had to compete with each other for food. One day, a stick emerged from the ground and started to talk in a strange humming sound. Only Yomimilu could understand what the stick was saying, and she didn't like the message. Still, as a lover of truth and protector of her people, she had to listen.

The stick told the animals which of them had to live by hunting and which by grazing. The animals didn't like it much, but obeyed. Then the stick told Yomimilu that the Spanish conquest would come one day. A Savior would appear to all people, Jesuscrusto. The Indians would see the savior more clearly than any other people on the earth, and the world would never be the same again.

Yomimilu told the Surem people what the stick had to say, but no one believed her. She got frustrated, then very angry and left the Surems, then headed North, bringing many of the rivers with her.

The Surem people thought about what Yomimilu had told them and started to believe it. Most of them buried themselves under the mountains or in the depths of the ocean. But a few Surems were brave enough to remain on the earth surface, prepared to face the future and turn a harsh thing into a good one. These brave people later became the Yaqui. And today, when the Yaqui need help, one of the Surem people emerged out from the mountains as spirits or from the ocean as whales, going back to their underground and underwater homes after giving the Yaqui what they need to stay alive.

It was a beautiful tale, well told yet another time to an audience that never tired of it. Charlie kept his distance from the listeners. His smile was deep, and it made sense that the tale was related at the time of his arrival, he thought.

Surems could, after all, take on the form of seeing-eye jackrabbits, gophers and mule deer. Changing the laws of time and space were child's play for these Spirit Helpers. Then again, the four legged guides who got Charlie through the desert mountains could have just been rabbits, gophers and mule deer, and his arrival due to intrinsic skill or dumb luck. It all depended on how you looked at it.

But pondering was not allowed here, whether it was to rest on laurels for past accomplishments or take refuge in guilt for past offenses and failures. Diane was inside the hospital hut, and would soon come out. Charlie knew all to well that the combatant who sets the time and place for confrontation always has the advantage, and he would need all the advantage he could get.

Charlie's entry into the Yaqui camp went unnoticed, to his shock, then his disappointment. Charlie was not used to indifference, having been spoiled by admiration and used to hatred. Who knew what awaited him once he entered the hospital he had built and then so abruptly abandoned?

As always, Charlie came with a plan. The sack of gifts over his back, combined with a cottonwood beard and a burlap-bag cap provided a workable Santa disguise for children who had never seen snow. He could maintain a jovial tone, as long as he kept talking, quickly and loudly. It would buy him time, maybe provide a laugh or two as well.

Diane and Charlie had shared a lot in earlier times, most particularly their common sense of humor. It was self-effacing, sarcastic and biting, all at the same time.

The clinic door opened with a bang as the Gringo Chris Kringle announced his arrival with a hearty ho-ho-ho, delivered with the intensity of a vaudevillian performer dedicated to the holy cause of Universal Irreverence. "Ho. Ho. Ho. I'm Santa. Flew in from the North Pole, and boy, are my arms real tired. Okay, the reindeer did all the work, but I was the one who had to convince them they could fly. Not easy for someone afraid to walk up a three-foot stepladder."

The jokes were in English, but their subtext was well understood, particularly by the children in the clinic. Charlie distributed gifts to each of them, objects worth barely a few cents each in Mexico City or San Antone, but the source of fascination to people so spoiled by living with what nature provided.

Mild chuckles, then loud laughs came out of the children's mouths. One bedridden girl smiled wider and more quietly than the others, the visitor from the North providing very much needed relief from abdominal surgery, that had to be performed to repair damage done by buckshot from the barrel of a nervous, triggerlight Federale recruit.

"Imagine the laughs I'd get if you understood what I was saying," Charlie said to the seven year old patient, gaining her trust in exchange for his courage to extend himself. "But we can't forget the special gift I have in my bag for the doctor."

Diane was removing gravel fragments from the arm of a Yaqui elder who overestimated his ability to handle a spooky horse, and underestimated the ability of rocks to tear open his flesh.

"Hello, Charlie," she said calmly, not allowing the rhythm of her hands to lose a beat, nor her eyes to look upon the man whom she could never stop thinking about for ten years, though each morning she kept trying.

From where Charlie stood, Diane was as beautiful as ever. Her naturally beautiful features were made more attractive by the added wrinkles on her sunbaked face, and the gray hairs which were rapidly dominating her three-foot long mane. Gone were the English and American clothes she brought down with her and refused to part with during the years she re-established her cultural roots here. Still present was her English accent, a crisp-sounding Oxfordian diction that could dig as sharp as a knife, and freeze the listener faster than a burst of Arctic Canadian wind.

"I...eh...got you something," Charlie babbled out of his quivering mouth, his optimistic mood deflated instantly by Diane's bitterness. He opened up the package, revealing a garment of traditional Yaqui design with the elegant, but simple trimmings.

"Thank you," Diane replied politely. "It's just what I need now." She smiled, then glanced up at Charlie, a cordial smile slowly forming on her face. Charlie's lips stopped shivering, and he breathed a deep sigh of relief. It was so easy, Charlie thought. Maybe she could read his repentant heart, and forgave him at a glance.

But Diane saw more than simple repentance. Much more. She tore up the dress, dumping the pieces into a basket. "We need bandages very badly these days, Charlie. Thank you."

Charlie knew he deserved a psychological beating on his rump, but not a whip cracked into his back. Then again, this was Diane's woodshed. She went back to work on the Yaqui elder's arm, ignoring Charlie. Being ignored was something that Charlie hated most, and she knew it.

All was not lost. The children still trusted Charlie, at least provisionally. He seemed sincere, and though Diane was the boss in medical matters here, she never forced other people to take on her vendettas.

Charlie wandered over to the girl with the abdominal surgery, admiring Diane's stitchery. "Interesting embroidery work. I got a lacerated heart that could use a whip-stitch like that to fix it."

Diane ignored the remark, fueled by an anger in her eyes that caused concern in the Yaqui gentleman under her care. His concern for her safety grew. He owed her for letting people think he was bucked off a feisty two year old stallion instead of getting kicked by a stubborn twenty-year old mare. Most importantly, she was family, and Charlie was now a stranger.

Charlie wandered over to a plaque on the wall, a framed degree from Harvard Medical School on it. With a sarcastic tone directed at institutions everywhere he commented, "Hey, I used to have one of these too. In case you want to pawn yours off, I can give you the address of an Okie rancher who'll give you a good price."

The remark would have elicited a laugh from Diane once, but not now. Maybe it was because she detected a dangerous kind of arrogance behind Charlie's sarcasm, the kind that was connected to forces that were more connected to power than wisdom.

"Unlike some people, I earned my degree," Diane replied, fueled by anger but controlled by reason. Her hands moved more abruptly, squeezing the elder's arm, her instruments pulling his flesh with the force of a Texas ranch hand yanking the family jewels off a steer calf at round-up.

Diane's remark struck an even deeper nerve in Charlie, for reasons he could not bring himself to tell her. His smart-assed smile disappeared, replaced by a look of unredeemable guilt.

"I had to claw my way to high school, college, and medical school," Diane shouted at Charlie in a soft, firm voice.

"Every administrator in New England wanted me on their hospital staff. And every one of their wives wanted my scalp on their flagpole."

"You beat us palefaces at our own game. You were good. Damn good," Charlie replied, with sincere admiration.

"So good that I almost forgot who I was, and where I came from," Diane countered. "I'm not going to let that happen again. Not even for you."

"It's been ten years," Charlie noted. "Things change."

"But you haven't," Diane replied with a directness Charlie couldn't ignore or deny. "You're still trying to 'liberate' the world. First it was with Villa down here, then against the Kaiser in Europe, then your Socialist street-revolts in London, New York and Chicago to free the 'ignorant working masses' from the evils of capitalism. It's always one more revolution with you, Charlie."

Apparently, Diane had been reading the letters Charlie sent, and was following his progress through the newspapers that filtered down from Texas and up from Mexico City. Charlie had asked for the political spotlight and he got it, along with Wentworth's unending wrath as part of the deal. Diane's biting remarks were accurate enough, but not completely truthful. She didn't care.

"You wanted to save the world as much as I did ten years ago," Charlie protested, trying to restrain his anger with the last reserves of his rapidly vanishing patience.

"And I'm still doing it," Diane replied loudly. "One person at a time."

Diane's tone silenced Charlie. It also pushed the concern of the Yaqui elder under Diane's scalpel blade into action. The old man gave Charlie a stern warning in Yaqui that did not require translation. Charlie backed off and reflected a moment, his silence allowing Diane to regain her perspective as she went about repairing the torn arteries, nerves, and ligaments in the old man's arms.

"We both came down here ten years ago to do something noble. To help these people and to help ourselves," Charlie said softly, with well spoken words coming from the heart.

Diane smiled, remembering better times with Charlie before the final Diaz dispersal, the Mexican Revolution, and the Great War to end all wars. They were years that challenged her spirit, but never broke it. If there was one thing that Diane and Charlie needed, it was challenge, and they were lucky enough to share far more than their share of happiness along with it.

"You look ten years younger than when I left," Charlie said, reading her thoughts and sharing the memories going through her head. He moved closer, feeling tempted to stroke her long mane.

"And you look twenty years older," she replied. It was a light-hearted put-off, but a put-off nevertheless. Charlie accepted it, grateful to be allowed the few liberties she was extending with him.

A wave of contentment overcame Diane. It soon spread, to the children, then the elder. He smiled in approval, thinking that she knew some redeeming thing about Charlie that no one else in the village did.

Diane had steady composure, as long as she was in control. She also had the steadiest surgical hands West of the Pecos, but something slipped. Her hand accidentally nicked a small vessel, releasing a small gush of blood. Her attention moved instantly to nip the bleeder, followed closely by Charlie's ever-watchful medical eye.

"Better watch that artery," Charlie commented, in a well-meaning but paternal tone.

"I am watching it," Diane replied, her apprehension accentuated by Charlie's unconsciously-delivered arrogance.

"And watch the nerve," Charlie continued.

"I'm watching the nerve too," Diane retorted quickly, with a quiet voice about to break into a scream.

Diane found a fragment of glass that had caused the problem and proceeded to pry it out. No once could do a better job than her, except of course, Charlie.

"Watch the way you pull on that fragment," he related. "If you go any more medially, you'll get a neuroma so bad that even I can't fix it."

"Charlie, I have everything under control," Diane grunted hrough gritted teeth, and a smile meant to keep the children calm, and her patient from tearing Charlie's head off with his good arm.

The Elder gave Charlie a sterner warning in his native tongue.

"What did he say," Charlie inquired of Diane, oblivious to the intensity of his subtext. "I'm a little rusty in Yaqui."

"You're a little rusty in a lot of things," Diane commented. As an American, Charlie was slow to pick up languages, and for varieties of reasons was particularly poor in his knowledge of the Yaqui language, even in the best of times.

The more Diane got flustered, the more blood gushed out of the Elder's arm. Charlie knew exactly what to do medically, but fell well short of the mark from the human perspective. He grabbed a spare scalpel and forceps and moved his way into the surgical field.

"Here. Let me show you a technique I developed at Yale, and did some modifications on when I was in Europe," he said, by way of commentary.

The Elder repeated the warning, but it was not understood or heeded. Charlie moved Diane aside to remove the hidden glass fragment from the Elder's arm, then found himself on the floor, the old man's bleeding arm on his neck. His good one was holding a stick.

He gave Charlie a final warning in simple words, undoubtedly describing what he would do to Charlie if he did not make a bee-line for Texas upon his release.

But the words were incomprehensible. Charlie was growing delirious, on his way to being someone very different than the jovial Santa who blew in from the North Pole. Meanwhile, the elder was getting weaker, the floor under his arm soaked with fresh blood. Charlie got more delirious as the elder got more determined.

The children gathered at one end of the room. Diane instinctively tried to protect them from something she knew was coming. Something she never saw, but always feared.

Charlie managed to make an escape from under the angry words of the Yaqui sexagenarian, but he was pursued, then pushed to the wall. The meshed bamboo and cottonwood framework held up, but Charlie's composure didn't. The second push into the wall pushed an intrinsic button in him which was connected to a very powerful energy source, putting his mind somewhere very far from the bucolic Yaqui River valley.

Charlie's combat instincts took over instantly, fueled by an intense hatred for himself and his combatants. He grabbed the old man and flung his two-hundred pound body across the room. The landing was hard, and Charlie's pursuit harder. The ex-super soldier kicked the old man around, forcing his face into the floor. Before the Yaqui Elder knew what had happened, Charlie pulled his hunting knife from its sheath and held it to the old man's throat.

"I'm not responsible for the bloodshed. And if you say any different, I'll kill you. So help me, I'll kill you," Charlie screamed out at the top of his lungs. "Leave me alone, leave me alone."

The old man was too drained to fight, but too proud to surrender. It was a look that scared Charlie, particularly when he realized that his opponent was not a ghost-skeleton embodied with demonic powers, but a man who happened to walk into Charlie's chronic, private nightmare.

"Yankee, go home," the Yaqui said to Charlie in plain English. They were the only three English words the old man knew, and the only ones needed. Speculators from California were coming down to Sonora every day now, attempting to establish profitable niches for themselves in the Yaqui valley, with the consent and support of President Obregon's military-industrial machine. Whatever history Charlie might have had here, he was now just another Gringo, a potential enemy who had to be watched, very closely.

"Charlie, I think it would be best for everyone if you leave now," Diane commented in a soft, rational voice. Her determination that the request be carried out was clearly demonstrated by the barrel of a *45 caliber shotgun* pointed at Charlie's head.

Her reluctance to make the request was clearly visible in her trembling, sweaty hands. Behind her were the children, seeking protection from the jovial Gringo Santa Claus who seemed to be possessed by demonic forces beyond their comprehension.

Charlie took a look at the faces of the frightened children who were his captive audience a short argument ago. He then took a look into himself.

Charlie let the old man up and knelt on the floor. The Elder delivered a mouthful of spit onto his face, then left, at Diane's request.

Eden had been destroyed, at least for Charlie. The rules dictated that destruction had to happen, and Charlie was tired of fighting the rules. He turned the knife in his hand upward and saw his reflection in its cold, hard steel. It was ugly, every feature of his handsome face deformed beyond recognition.

Myriads of images and voices went through his mind as he prepared to plunge the tip of the razor-sharp blade into his heart, his knowledge of medical anatomy still functional enough to know how to penetrate the rib cage quickly and cleanly. Diane could only see someone who was beyond the help of any mortal man or woman.

Charlie muttered the Lord's Prayer through his quivering lips. Diane knelt down beside him, laying the shotgun barrel down, but keeping its trigger in easy reach.

"Charlie, please give me the knife," she requested, with a pervading calmness in her very directed voice.

The request was heard, but not heeded. Charlie prayed louder and shut his eyes as hard as he could. Diane laid down the gun and moved her hand onto Charlie's shoulder.

The touch was light, but effective. Charlie turned around, defending himself against the intruder from the world of the living with the fear of a child being stalked by the most fearful creatures of his imagination. "Charlie," Diane repeated. Her voice firm and stead, she moved closer. A look at Diane's face somehow made Charlie drop the knife and come back from the nightmare that kept haunting his every waking hour since his alliance with Wentworth.

"Charlie," she said with fear and compassion. "I don't know what demons are haunting you, and I hope you can get rid of them one day. But I think it would be wise, all around, if you leave. Please."

Charlie knew that Diane was right. She would have given the world to be wrong. Another practitioner would be needed to cure Charlie's disease-ridden soul.

He took a last look at the hospital around him, admiring the medical devices that bore O'Brien numbers. Those inventions did much to save lives here, but could never do so through his hands again.

Charlie worked his way around the children huddled in the corners and slowly walked to the doorway. He made one more request to take a final look around. It was denied, affirmed by Diane's answering with a loaded shotgun in her shaking hands.

The footsteps Charlie took on the ground outside the hospital hut felt hard on his feet, rattling every bone in his body. The door slammed shut behind him, digging a knife into his heart. That heart was still alive, even though he was so skilled in the various ways to kill it.

The ride home would be hard, particularly since Charlie didn't know where home was now. West Texas would do, or perhaps New Mexico would provide a haven for a loner biding out his time, until he was lucky enough to be taken out by a hungry grizzly's teeth or a bounty hunter's bullet.

Charlie rode quietly up to the mountain trail leading to the Bacatete plateaus. He glanced behind him and saw the fiery blue-eyed boy who had inherited his genes but not his name. Carlos was being pulled into the hospital building against his will by Diane, undoubtedly for a heart to heart talk with the boy which she hoped to postpone for several more years, or perhaps permanently.

A glance at Carlos was all Charlie needed to see how things were, and feel how painful they could get. He rode on, recalling the classical poetic phrase, "no man's an island." He had successfully rebutted that 17th century hypothesis many times against less academically-skilled opponents.

At the very least, Charlie needed purpose; continuing his ongoing battle with Wentworth seemed as good a purpose as any other. But without anyone to share the victory with, it would be an empty one. And warriors without countries to go home to rarely emerged from battles victorious or alive.

Chapter 8

Brisk winds picked up from the Southwest, blowing through the trees and low lying bush with gusts that came up and diminished without warning. Charlie's mind could envision banshees sweeping across the desert pushing him onward to a final confrontation with death or, worse, an uneventful life as a has-been who would never-be again.

It was rare for Charlie's steed to be spooked at something as simple as wind, but nothing was simple in the Bacatete foothills, particularly the wind.

Charlie's attempts to calm the horse only made it more afraid. To the steed, and to Charlie, the eagles seemed like vultures and the lizards like snakes who sprouted legs. The horse made a quick getaway; Charlie took a hard fall.

Charlie shook the brains back into his head, and spit the dust out of his mouth. He hobbled over to a ride, seeing the horse nibbling on a patch of green grass growing amidst the sage and tumbleweeds a few hundred yards away.

"Come on. There's plenty of grass up North.. Come on," Charlie said as he edged his way closer to the horse. But the steed had other ideas, either out of independence, or the desire to teach Charlie a lesson, keeping a stride ahead of Charlie's hands, two if he tried to grab the reins.

Finally, after a mile or two, the horse stood still. Charlie approached slowly, and gently reached for the reins, only to have them ripped out of his hands as the horse galloped away over the hills, into a holler and over the ridge towards a higher plateau.

The sun rose a few degrees higher in the sky, heating up Charlie's boiling temper. Enough was enough. A few more attempts to catch the horse produced the same result, leaving him on tired feet behind an animal that knew it had the upper hand and was reluctant to give it up.

The walk over to the next valley humbled Charlie, despite his efforts to fight it. His anger was diffused by the drudge through the soft sand, and his troubled mind was exhausted by the hot sun. The desert does that, putting things into perspective whether you want things put into perspective or not.

The horse kept going North, leaving a clear enough trail to follow. Then it left no trail at all. Then, at the moment of ultimate hopelessness, a break in the gloom - a gift the desert gives those with blind persistence.

The horse appeared on the horizon, standing tall and proud. A four foot-tall individual holding its reins. It could be one of the Surem people come up from the earth to help him on his way, Charlie thought, as he tried to make out the details of the ominous silhouette. A closer look revealed something even more profound.

Carlos was always good at making friends with wild things, and Charlie's horse was as wild as they came in the ways that mattered. How the boy had traveled so far on foot Charlie could only imagine. Perhaps Carlos had inherited some of his father's super-skills in his legs. Or perhaps Charlie had been traveling in circles, certainly nothing new for him in these foothills.

But it didn't matter. Charlie was grateful to see his horse and his son. "Thank you," he said to Carlos in Spanish, "He's a smart horse. It takes a very smart person to catch him," he continued.

But Carlos understood little Spanish and virtually no English, a byproduct of Diane's trying to seclude him from the world that gave her so much professional success, then so much personal tragedy. But Carlos was half-Yaqui and, as such, an expert at subtext in any language.

The boy smiled, allowing Charlie to reach for the reins. Just as Charlie's hands grasped hold of the leather, Carlos' smile turned angry. He gave the horse a command in Yaqui, and the animal bolted off into the valley below.

The horse stopped just shy of a patch of wild timothy grass, as if commanded to do so by his new four-foot tall Yaqui friend and master. Carlos screamed a stream of angry Yaqui words at Charlie, then turned to the Southern sky for a long walk home.

Charlie understood few of the words, but all of their meanings. Carlos' anger and disappointment hurt Charlie in a place inside him that he never felt before. A whole universe inside Charlie's disillusioned heart opened up. A void of emptiness that would consume him forever unless something was done about it, here and now.

Begging was something Charlie swore never to do. He operated on the famous Western credo that a real man didn't lie, cheat or apologize. Another unwritten rule for rugged individualists was to never reveal your true feelings to anyone. As long as there was something that your enemies and friends didn't know about you, your survival was ensured.

All of those codes would have to be severely modified if Charlie was going to get Carlos' understanding, approval and forgiveness. Charlie would need all three to regain some purpose to his life.

For Charlie, catching up to Carlos was almost as difficult as keeping up with his horse. The boy was accustomed to running through the desert, the soles of his feet having been baked by the sun and blistered so many times that only a razor-sharp steel blade could penetrate the skin. Charlie's physique was consistent with a well-conditioned Olympic racer, but his muscles were more suited to spurring on a horse, or balancing his weight on a motorcycle, than for running long distances in the mountains. He was good at the sprints, a byproduct of having survived many combat skirmishes, but gave out after the first two hundred yards.

"Wait, I want to talk to you. Please," Charlie screamed out to Carlos, in as many languages as he could remember, from the base of his winded lungs.

Carlos kept running up a rocky plateau, then down into a canyon blanketed by cactus and cottonwood, and populated with snakes and lizards that did not take kindly to uninitiated human trespassers.

The only way for Charlie to catch up was to jump and cut off Carlos at the mountain pass that led to the village. The descent would break Charlie's neck if taken wrongly. To remain on the plateau would leave him far more injured. His mind felt the presence of ghosts from his past, waiting to drop a net on him and extract vengeance for the many crimes Charlie had committed in the name of compassion.

It was the nightmare that invaded Charlie's dreams, but with some notable differences. The desert below was hard rock, not the Atlantic ocean. There was no escape boat waiting for him once he hit the rock-hard surface. What's more, Carlos, not

Diane, seemed to be the link to the Promised Land, where sins could be cleansed and death turned into life.

A few more futile screams of desperation from Charlie only made Carlos run more quickly. The boy could not be convinced by words, so Charlie took appropriate action. A leap off the plateau put the heroic Gringo into the air in a perfectly timed dive. The nature of the landing was less dramatic, and far more painful, leaving Charlie with a pulled hamstring and an appreciable degree of discomfort in his seldom-used, but highly-rated genitalia.

"Carlos, listen to me . . . Please," Charlie pleaded with a desperation he had never revealed to anyone. "I need you to understand why I had to leave, and why I had to come back." The words were in English, but the meaning was understood.

"Why?" said Carlos. "Why" was one of the only Yaqui words Charlie remembered, maybe because he had used it so often.

"I went away to fight a war in Europe. If I won that war, it would end all wars. That was the promise," Charlie said in broken Yaqui, Spanish and English. The words had a stutter that felt foreign to his usually sharp and witty tongue. He was out of control, a victim to his feelings. And if there was one thing Charlie couldn't control, it was his feelings.

Carlos looked at Charlie with anger, then pity, as the hero of the Great War and the Socialist Revolution sank to his knees, desperately pleading his case. Dissatisfied with the repetition of answers that were accurate, but not the truth, Carlos turned away and proceeded to walk home. The boy was completely unaware of the anguish that tormented Charlie's every waking thought since his alliance with Wentworth. Still, Charlie hoped that someone would - or could.

"Come back here," Charlie screamed through a parched throat. He grabbed Carlos by the shoulder, forcing the boy to listen. "Look. You may not understand what's going on inside me, and I pray to God you never do. But I care about you. And I always want you to know that."

Charlie pulled out his compass, placing it in Carlos' hand. The boy looked at it with curiosity. Knowledge of the four directions was intrinsic to every Yaqui, but designating them on a round dial with numbers and letters seemed odd to a youth so in tune with the natural cycles of the sun, moon and stars.

"Look at this 'N' here. Up there," Charlie said in a compassionate voice that won Carlos' heart - or at least his undivided attention. "I know that your place is here, and that my place is up there. If you ever want to find me, use this." Charlie shed a tear of sweet sorrow. Carlos cracked a smile.

"But don't use this compass in the Bacatetes," Charlie continued with a lifted spirit, remembering how magnetic North kept shifting on him in that mystical high country. "If you get lost up there, ask the rabbits and gophers for directions."

It was a strange joke, but surprisingly one which was understood. The sincerity behind it was reinforced by a hug from Charlie, a gesture with which the Gringo super-hero was never very comfortable. It felt uneasy at first, most of the energy going in one direction. But Carlos gave enough back to make Charlie feel good about his future, wherever it was going to be.

"Now," Charlie said. "You didn't see my horse around here?" he continued in broken Yaqui.

With a whistle from Carlos, the animal came galloping in and stopped abruptly at his feet. Charlie was amazed at his son's intuitive skills. He was also frightened. So much insight and super ability could backfire one day.

Sensing Charlie's apprehension, Carlos showed Charlie a patch of grass, its aroma being bait used by the Yaqui to catch horses since the time of the Spanish. Charlie smiled, embarrassed and relieved.

Charlie grabbed the reins and reacquainted himself with the horse. He mounted up and looked up to the Bacatete slopes. Suddenly, he felt a tug on the reins, and the impulse of the animal moving to the southwest. A look over the steed's head revealed Carlos pulling the horse onward, talking up a storm in a cheerful tone that suited the Yaqui tongue.

"But, your mother. She doesn't want me around," Charlie said, somehow finding the words to make himself clearly understood.

"She will," Carlos said.

"We're both going to be in deep shit when we get back there," Charlie said. He translated the phrase into the most respectable

Yaqui he could remember.

Carlos' response was more graphic, initiating a conversation using vulgar language and the most jovial of tones. Father and son had rediscovered each other, filling a hole that neither Carlos or Charlie knew was there until only a few hours ago.

Carlos' persistence came from the genes provided by Diane and Charlie, and was reinforced by his traditional, but somewhat improvised, Yaqui upbringing. The sight of an angry Diane and well-armed Yaqui warriors in front of the clinic door would not prevent Charlie's reunion with Diane, if Carlos had anything to say about it.

"Charlie, get out of here," Diane said firmly.

"This was Carlos' idea," Charlie rebutted.

"Carlos," Diane said. "Get out of the way."

The Yaqui warriors aimed their weapons at Charlie's head, preparing to do whatever was required to ensure Diane's safety. Charlie may have given them modern medical technology and indispensable military aid during the revolution, but Diane gave them something much more valuable.

Carlos brought the horse in, tying it to the post. He proceeded to start an argument with Diane at a pace too rapid for Charlie to understand. It was not usual for a Yaqui child to be so openly argumentative with his parents, but Carlos was an unusual child, born under unusual circumstances.

The Yaqui warriors kept their guns steady. Charlie tried to do the same with his troubled mind. This was a situation that could not be negotiated. Carlos was his lawyer, Diane his judge, and the warriors his executioners, in the event of a guilty verdict. Just as Diane was about to overrule Carlos' last objection to the trial proceedings, an Elder stepped out from behind a willow.

He had watched Charlie's eyes and knew Diane's heart. His face was familiar to Charlie, though he could not figure out why or how. Dreams, nightmares, and visions seemed irrelevant now.

An elder story-teller stepped into view of everyone, silencing the argument immediately. Diane stated her case to the old man, openly speaking her mind. He listened, contemplated, then allowed Carlos his turn, giving the boy the same respect as his mother.

After both cases were heard, the elder moved closer to Charlie. There was a fire in the old man's eyes, emanating an energy which did not need power to be expressed. The old curandero could place himself into the moccasins, sandals or cowboy boots of most anyone, instantly knowing what that person was thinking, feeling, and what their life was and would probably be. Even Charlie couldn't put up a lead shield to the Elder's x-ray vision.

After a long five second stare, the Elder gave the verdict, in favor of the defendant. The warriors lowered their weapons and went on their way. Carlos gave Charlie a thumbs up, a disgruntled Diane behind him.

Charlie dismounted and approached Diane, taking his blanket and gear off the saddle. "So, where do I -"

"Down by the river," Diane said abruptly. "Grass for your horse, an old hut for you. We start work at the clinic at sunrise. A set of rules will be posted."

With her ultimatum delivered, Diane walked into the hospital, bolt locking the door behind her.

Charlie looked around him, contented for the first time in a long while. It was a strange emotion, and he did not know how to accept the obligations that came with it. But he was eager to learn.

He noticed Carlos by the horse, forging a bond with the animal that defied description by any words in English, in terms of its depth and inner significance. Charlie invited Carlos to come with him to his assigned dwelling.

As soon as the offer was accepted, Diane screamed out from behind the hospital walls, demanding Carlos' presence. Not being greedy about his victories, Carlos handed over the reins to Charlie and went into the clinic.

Charlie walked the horse toward the river. He remembered the old Negro prospector in Tiens, digging his own fortune and dignity with a shovel, singing Lincoln's old Negro Spiritual Hymn with the joy of a slave finally liberated from bondage by his own efforts. The nightmare was finally over. The dream could be resurrected or, failing that, rebuilt anew. So he thought. So he hoped.

Chapter 9

Days passed, then weeks, then months. Charlie had built enough huts outside the hospital to house the entire Yaqui nation, and then some. More importantly, he built a door into Diane's heart. More important than that, he built a door to his own Salvation.

It took a few weeks of prodding from the Yaqui elders, but Diane finally let Charlie into the hospital in a professional capacity. Charlie was a more effective healer now than he had ever been. He thoroughly enjoyed working with, under, and for the Yaqui medicine men. No medical suggestion was dismissed because of its sole identity with wilderness or the laboratory. The word holistic truly applied to this place, once again. It seemed that even death itself could be defeated here.

In a surprising turn of events, death had seemed to take a holiday in Sonora itself during the Spring of that year. Obregon would be running for reelection soon, and decided to make trouble for his political opponents in Mexico City, rather than for the Yaqui. The promises of land and liberty for the Yaqui had still not delivered, but the Mexican soldiers stationed in Sonora stayed further away from Yaqui warriors in public places. Perhaps that fear would turn into respect. At least there was less shooting. Men could hunt. Women could farm. Children could experience a spring without bloodshed.

Carlos was growing up to be a man, but on his own terms. Charlie tried to teach Carlos how to be a doctor, but the inclinations of the boy were still to enjoy life, rather than to battle death. Diane saw the wisdom in this. She also saw the wisdom of becoming intimate with Charlie.

As Diane and Charlie became closer with each other, they found themselves getting more involved with the Yaqui communities. These involvements were about play as well as work, and seemed to bring out the best of Charlie's abilities.

Of the few pleasant memories Charlie remembered from his younger days, playing stickball was the most prominent. Dreaming was the American obsession, but baseball was the American pastime. Charlie was an American, and it was Springtime. The Yaqui were short on anything that resembled baseball equipment, but they did have something that would make playing the game more interesting - donkeys.

Charlie heard about donkey baseball while traveling through Oklahoma, but he never saw it. Perhaps Charlie was just being fed a tall tale by an Okie who wanted to get the last laugh on a Northerner with a strange accent. But, he would find out soon enough.

It was Sunday afternoon in Vicom. For two days, Charlie had been busy converting a fallow bean field into the first regulation baseball diamond in the Yaqui valley, in time for opening day of the Yaqui donkey baseball season. Yaqui Indians from Vicom and several of the adjacent towns gathered to participate in this new game introduced by the eccentric Gringo. Charlie had paid his dues for such a privilege. In the spirit of give and take, he had participated in several informal Yaqui competitions, and enjoyed coming in last in most every event.

But now it was Charlie's turn to deal the hand. He was proudly mounted on a donkey, on top of a pile of dirt which he designated as the pitcher's mound. He announced the rules of the game in an honest, though ineffective, attempt to translate baseball slang into the Yaqui language. Diane did her best to retranslate the words more accurately to the crowd of smiling Yaqui players waiting to take the field. The catcher and batter were to be on foot. Everyone else was to be on donkeys, chosen at random. An unexpected complication was that somehow, a few of the animals had some access to loco weed earlier that day.

Charlie lifted up his hand, threw a handmade ball of rubber and deerhide, and bellowed out, "Play ball!" The donkey spooked, tossing Charlie into the dust. The crowd laughed. Charlie laughed even harder. Then, he noticed two unexpected visitors behind the crowd. He squinted his eyes, thinking that the sun was playing tricks with his mind again.

John Smith and Emma Wentworth stood tall behind the crowd, and greeted Charlie with wide smiles and loud voices. Emma had taken to wearing a safari hat, upon which were well earned souvenirs of the various places she had experienced in the last year. Around John's neck was a new camera. The understated confidence in his eyes indicated that he had already taken a lifetime of photographs with it. These two idealists had indeed become journalists, who were both observers and participants in their stories. Apparently, they had gotten word about opening day of the Yaqui baseball league, and planned their arrival for this moment. Charlie obliged them by inviting them to play. The young Gringos eagerly accepted, and joined forces with the newly formed Potam Eagles against Charlie's Vicom Hawks. The Indians didn't take this game as passionately as Charlie did, but since it was important to Charlie, it became important to them.

The first batter up was a warrior from Potam, wielding a bat which had been a branch of a large cottonwood tree barely an hour ago. He was determined to hit the ball out of the park, all the way to the Arizona border. His bulging biceps gave ample evidence that he was capable of the task.

Charlie was on the mound, holding the reins of his donkey with his teeth. He wound up and threw. "Strike one," shouted Diane from behind home plate. Charlie's Hawks cheered. The visiting Potam Eagle bench jeered with equal enjoyment. Charlie spit on the ball, sized up the batter's stance, and stopped himself before he did the customary scratch of the crotch. He wound up, threw, and landed a fast ball into the catcher's mitt, a heavily reinforced leather glove worn by Diane.

"Ball one," yelled out Diane in her official capacity as Umpire. The Eagle and Hawk benches responded appropriately. Charlie protested as loudly and vehemently as any coach in the big leagues up north. Diane calmly threw the ball back to him and repeated the call.

At the count of three and two, the mules were getting restless, and everyone was in the spirit of the game. The pitch came, then the swing. The ball was hit, and hit hard. It flew up in the air and spiraled down to the ground, as the deerskin seams were beginning to break. The batter looked up at the shattered ball in amazement.

Diane nudged him, as a reminder of his cue to run the bases. The Potam warrior got on his donkey and kicked it onward to first base. The left outfielder retrieved the ball and ran his mule to the infield, then tossed what was left of the ball to the first baseman. But it was too late. The runner was on his way to second. He jumped off his donkey at second base and held on to the sack of beans that designated its spot. "Safe," yelled out Diane, as both sides cheered the runner for his accomplishment.

The next batter was a pregnant woman from Potam. The way she handled the bat indicated that she had previous experience with the game. Charlie protested to the Umpire that one of the rules of donkey baseball was that pregnant women aren't allowed to play. Diane reminded Charlie that the Umpire can change the rules of donkey baseball anytime he or she wanted to. The woman asked Diane if it would be alright if her son could run the bases for her. Charlie agreed to the arrangement, then regretted his decision, as he saw a six foot two Yaqui with a physique that would rival a Greek god emerge from the crowd.

Charlie threw the first ball. It was a hit, and a foul. The next throw was a hit into the infield. The shortstop galloped into the infield, turned his donkey around on a dime, then threw to the man on third. The crowd cheered the fielders.

It was two on, and nobody out. John was up. He had seen enough baseball games in his recent travels through the States to know that a good hitter is not only accurate with a bat, but proficient at intimidating the pitcher. He knocked the dirt from his shoes with the makeshift bat and put some chewing tobacco in his mouth. He took a few chews, then spit on the bat. This was followed by adjusting his pants, moving the visor on his hat. He then indulged in whatever other cliched baseball ritualistic gestures he could do in mixed company.

Next to John was Emma, trying to restrain his donkey as the animal insisted on kicking at every real or imaginary thing in sight.

"Charlie, I think this is gonna be dangerous," commented Emma.

"Naw," intervened John in a loud Texas twang that frustrated the listener by its slowness of delivery. "I'm gonna hit the ball so far outta here that I'll have time to build a wagon, hitch that mule to the wagon, then promenade all around this park. Three times."

Charlie could handle a face-off with anyone, but he could never be patient. After John thwarted his attempts to wind up for the pitch 8 times, Charlie yelled out frustrated, "Are ya through!!!"

"Hey, I'm ready," replied John calmly, with a self assured smile.

Charlie and John stared each other down, enjoying the thrill of a showdown which did not involve killing or humiliation. They grimaced, then growled. Diane and Emma looked at each other with a "men will be boys" look.

Finally there was a pitch, a swing and a miss. "Strike One," yelled Diane. Charlie smiled with satisfaction, then looked around him to see the runner at second moving toward third, and prepared to throw the ball to the shortstop and tag the runner "out." The shortstop tapped the runner on the shoulder in a friendly manner, reminding him that it would be best if he returned to second. The runner complied.

Charlie cleared his throat and faced John one more time. The tension mounted as the two Gringos prepared for their next joust in what was their own private tournament. Then Charlie let out his fast ball. A swing, then a bang. John had driven the ball into the mountain meadows behind the outfield. He gloated as Charlie threw his glove on the ground in frustration. A Yaqui handed John the reins of his donkey.

John got on the animal, prepared to promenade around the bases like a hero, but the loco weed the donkey had ingested earlier made it unresponsive to both rider and reality. It took one bucking hop toward first base, then hightailed it to third. The rider-runner approaching home from third was tossed off his donkey. The ball came into the infield, and the runner was tagged "out." John was still mounted and insisted that the donkey turn around. But since the animal had an inverted perception of the universe, it assumed that John wanted it to speed on toward second, and then to first. A second rider-runner was thrown off his donkey, knocked to the ground, then tagged "out." John's mule then set out on a course toward home, past second, then first.

By this time, the game had turned into a marvelously chaotic festival. John's donkey saw home plate, then reared up. John was tossed off and found himself with his face in the mud, his left foot firmly planted on home. He was enthusiastically greeted by both the Eagles and the Hawks. Even Diego, the hard edged "bronco" rebel, cracked a smile.

Emma extended her hand to John, welcoming him into the joke. She hugged him, then kissed him on the cheek. The couple turned around to see Diane put a “minus one” score on for John’s team. Both sides applauded the ruling.

Chapter 10

Since the state of Sonora was founded in the 1820s, the Yaqui had a reputation amongst the Mexican settlers of being wild savages. These Indians had a fire which could not be quenched. This fire found its way into the way the Yaqui conducted war. It also found its way into the way the Yaqui conducted their religious ceremonies.

The Yaqui considered themselves devoted Christians. Their passion for life was displayed most profoundly and most intensely in worship of their master and friend Jesus Christ. There was fervor and passion in this worship. It was displayed openly and on a mass scale. Perhaps this was one of the reasons why the Yaqui were considered so dangerous. A mirror is one of the most frightening things to a Catholic who is not living a Christian life. And perhaps the Yaqui represented such a mirror to the very Catholic country of Mexico.

The Spring of 1926 was a good time. It was also the season for the most sacred and joyous of Yaqui holidays, La Fiesta de Gloria. It was merely Easter in the Mexican part of Sonora.

It was appropriate that Charlie and Diane were living near Vicom, and that John and Emma stayed on to observe life here from a vantage point not allowed any journalists before them.

It was Wednesday of Holy Week. The passion play of Christ's coming to Jerusalem, the Crucifixion, and the Resurrection were dramatized on the streets of Vicom, and the inhabitants of the town were the players. Yaqui came in from everywhere, mostly on foot, carrying with them only the food they would need for the four days ahead.

The fiesta started with the beating of the drum. Then a lighting of the candles on the church altar.

Then came the devil chasers, donning their distinctive wardrobe. A blanket secured by a deer hoof belt covered his chest. On their feet were cocoon-rattler anklets. They marched around the village while their spokesman delivered a sermon, answered periodically with "amens" from the crowd, each holding a candle with the utmost dedication.

Then, without warning, the solemn crowd went into a mad frenzy, women pulled their skirts up behind their backs, screeching at the top of their lungs, louder than drunken whores in a Texas cathouse. Men beat each other with whips upon their bare backs, till the ground under their feet turned beet red. Then, the bedlam stopped, candles were relit. Solemn worshippers gathered at the church. Then silence became madness as they bellowed like calves, howled like coyotes, screeched like owls. Tribute was given to nature, Christ and the Church.

Then, quiet again, the worshippers retired to their homes or campfires, in preparation for the next day's festivities. The nightwatch would be kept by the devil dancers.

The night was warm, a gentle breeze coming up from the Sea of Cortez. Emma watched the festival with fascination. John eyed it with less childlike emotions.

John saw a devil dancer wearing an animal mask kneel down, cross himself at the crucifix on the altar, then dance around it to the rapid beat of a drum and accompanying flute. "These Injuns's Christian?" he asked Charlie.

"They are," Charlie replied, proudly.

Emma interjected, "The dances, the songs, they seem, I don't know, they're..."

"Pagan," John responded in an indignant manner. Charlie smelled the ugly odor of American bigotry. He could never walk away from it in the States, and he would not tolerate it down here.

"They're honoring the spirit of the Earth," Diane interjected, anticipating Charlie's anger and with an understanding of John's ignorance. "They honor God's presence in all living things. What we call nature. It's a very basic Christian concept. Honor the earth and you honor yourself."

"I don't recall nothin' like that from Bible classes in Texas," John retorted.

"This ain't Texas," Charlie replied. With that, he turned around and went to sleep.

John gazed up at the stars above and wrapped a blanket around him. He didn't sleep that night, fearing that he would be scalped by one of the "hethens" below if he let his guard down. John showed little fear in the face of physical danger from police, militia or mobsters in the last year's travels through seven states, three Canadian provinces, and two banana republics. But this was another country, with players that dwelt in the world of the spirit. Indeed, the Yaqui valley was a different planet during the Fiesta de la Gloria.

The next day's festivities proceeded as scheduled. Upon the ringing of the morning bell from the Church tower, Christ was captured by the Romans and the Pharisees. The Romans, dressed in Mexican garb, marched in columns, very official.

The Pharisees, best known as Chapayekas, wore blankets over their chests, trousers, cocoon rattles around their ankles, and had very characteristic masks on their heads. They walked around like blind fools, communicating with each other by beating two sticks together.

The Romans had been "occupying" the town of Vicom for weeks. The Chapayekas had been spying on the townspeople for at least as long, trying the best they could to scare the children. Adults played along with the dream, and children learned how to respond to the Chapayekas on their own terms.

The role of Christ was an honored, but challenging one. The man elected to it had to have experience in the ways of the world and an insight into the depths of the spirit. He was to walk barefoot along the rocky streets, bearing a heavy cross, and be whipped across his naked back. In more masochistic times, Charlie would have killed for the role. Diane made him content to watch a more deserving man play the part.

By nightfall, the wounded Christ was locked up in a Roman jail, the power of the Virgin Mary was stolen, and all that remained to protect the altar, the symbol of the Holy Spirit, were the Soldier Angels and the Masobuikame, the Deer Dancers.

The angels were played by children from the village, using their innocence to protect the shimmering light of good from the powerful forces of evil. The Deer Dancers represented the huya aniya, and accessed its power by dancing and chanting.

As the drama of the Passion Play increased, nature offered its assistance by making it feel all the more real. The night air took on a cold chill, and wind bursts came from all directions. The Romans and Chapayekas attacked the altar with fervor, but were held off valiantly by the Soldier Angels and the Deer Dancers.

Carlos was not cast as a Soldier Angel, but he was as absorbed as any other Yaqui in the passion of the moment. Charlie and

Diane chose to keep him close by as they watched the attacks take place throughout the night.

Emma was quickly developing an understanding for the ceremonies, and for the reason why Charlie was so obsessed with returning here. John found himself jumping in fright from Chapayekas as much as any of the Yaqui children around him. Soon, the disbelieving John found himself actually rooting for the "good angels."

The group of Gringos moved closer to the altar to get a better look at the battle between good and evil. Behind them a group of Chapayekas, trying to scare them away. John grabbed Emma. Protecting Emma made John feel safe, even though she hardly needed protection in this strange and wonderful village. Carlos yelled back at the Chapayekas. They ran away. Carlos pursued.

Charlie smiled with pride. The masks and gestures were more frightening than ever this year, but Carlos did not show the slightest bit of fear.

Diane turned to Charlie, folded her arms and asked, "Did you tell Carlos what the Chapayekas had up their sleeve this year?"

"Hey. Carlos is a brave kid," Charlie replied. "He's doing all this on his own." Charlie's eyes remained fixed on the sight of his four foot tall son chasing away seven foot tall demons into the night horizon.

Diane looked at Charlie's eyes to see if his comments were truthful. They seemed to be.

Still, Charlie was learning the art of mischief, particularly playful mischief. Emma joined in with Diane in assessing the validity of his claim.

"What are you looking at?" he commented in his defense, in a gentle self-effacing manner.

"Nothing," replied Diane and Emma in unison. They turned around and proceeded to ignore Charlie, something which they both knew would frustrate him.

John looked around him. Carlos was missing, nothing unusual for Carlos. Charlie, Emma and Diane called out for him, but their voices could not be heard amidst the clamorous sounds of the battle between good and evil going on behind them. They split up to look for him. The fireworks symbolizing the triumph of life over death would be shot into the moonless sky soon, and it would be fitting that it be celebrated together, as a family.

Nature had provided a particular darkness to that night. The sky was moonless and clouds were coming in, hiding the view of the stars. Carlos' chase of the Chapayekas took him to a remote area of town. At the edge of the railway station, the Chapayekas split up and ran into the hills. But one remained.

He was the largest, and had the fiercest mask. He called for his assistants with his sticks, but they did not show up. Carlos pursued further, into a blind alley. The Chapayeka was cornered, facing a wall of sunbaked clay twenty feet tall on all sides.

Carlos told the Chapayeka to leave and never return. But Carlos had cornered something - and someone - much more powerful than any Chapayeka or Roman Centurion.

The Chapayeka turned around. His blanket turned into a black cape, and his three point Yaqui sandals into spit polished cavalry boots, with sharp spurs drenched in blood. The face matched the wardrobe.

Wentworth approached Carlos, inviting the boy to come with him.

Carlos had never met Wentworth. Charlie never told his son about him. Wentworth was Charlie's albatross. He would spend an eternity in hell before linking Carlos to him. Wentworth's voice was warm, inviting, and would seem sincere to most boys. But Carlos was not most boys. He was Charlie's son, and he was a Yaqui. .

As if he knew that these two affiliations would mean certain death by Wentworth in hand, Carlos ran toward the exit of the alley as fast as he could. The lad could run up any mountain in the Bacatetes with both hands tied behind his back. But atop every escape route in the valley was a Mexican soldier armed with a repeater rifle and a fixed bayonet.

Carlos found a rope and made a run for a steep wall leading to a tower that overlooked the desert. He tossed the rope up to the top and climbed up as fast as he could. Just as he could see an escape route into the desert, a bootheel pushed him down to the hard ground.

Carlos was knocked unconscious. Wentworth gently picked the boy up off the ground. An Army Captain rode by. Wentworth put his cape over the boy's torso, kissed him on the cheek, then handed him over to the officer.

"You know where to take him," said Wentworth to the Captain. "I will be joining you directly."

The Captain gave a snappy salute and moved on. His men mounted their horses and followed him into the darkness of the desert. Their horses moved fast but quietly.

Wentworth looked at his watch, then moved on. There was still one more important item of business of his very hidden agenda.

Diane was closer to Carlos than anyone. It was only natural that her sixth sense would lead her to look for him in this area of town. It was also natural that Wentworth could find her there. Diane called out Carlos' name several times. Wentworth appeared out of the dark with a pipe, whistling "God Save the King."

"I say, do you have a match?" Wentworth asked politely. Diane had never seen Wentworth before, but she knew that any stranger in this area of the country should be considered an enemy unless proven otherwise. This is particularly true if that man is an Anglo, with an accent from her home country across the Atlantic.

"I say, do you have a match? Wentworth repeated.

"No. I don't," replied Diane nervously.

"Pity," Wentworth replied.

Wentworth turned and started to walk away, singing the verses of "God Save the King" with an angelic baritone voice that sent shrills down Diane's spine.

She turned around and walked away slowly, then sped up as quickly as she dared. Then she was overcome with an unexpected feeling of being at ease, for reasons she could not understand. Stranger things were known to happen to people during the Fiesta de la Gloria.

Diane smiled and thought upon fond childhood memories in England. Her head was held high and she started to hum "God Save the King," then to sing it. Her mind's eye could smell steak and kidney pie, freshbaked scones, and the flowers by the River Thames which blossomed this time of year. Then she heard her name, "Diane," in the voice of her departed father.

She turned around. Wentworth repeated Diane's name in her father's voice, lifted a pistol from underneath his coat, and shot her. It was a clear shot, directly between her hazel blue eyes.

It was also a well timed shot. The fireworks signaled the victory of the Soldier Angels and the Deer Dancers over the Romans and Chapayekas. Good had triumphed over evil in the town square. The Resurrection of Christ was complete. But there would be two less people who would be around to celebrate it this year.

Chapter 11

The Yaqui took great pains to pay tribute to those who passed on, and Diane's funeral was no exception to this time- honored custom. The ritual lasted three days and nights, and was carried out with as much passion as the Fiesta de la Gloria. John and Emma stayed to honor the dead. Charlie left to get revenge on the living. Wentworth would pay a high price for taking Diane's life. The British industrialist would pay an even higher price for kidnapping Carlos. If Carlos was dead, not even the devil's own armor could protect Wentworth from Charlie's rage.

Wentworth's riders left a clear trail out of Vicom. It coursed along the Sea of Cortez, then hugged the rocky slopes of the Bacatete high country. It was the kind of country where a pursuer could be seen for miles and be picked off at leisure by even the poorest marksman.

From the Bacatete badlands he saw new railroad tracks on the flat below him. Foreign investors had put a lot of money into this line, and President Obregon was determined that it be a successful enterprise. It was reelection time in Northwest Mexico. Railroads brought in many votes, and Obregon needed all the votes he could get in this election year. Sonora also had resources wanted by Obregon's silent partners - gold, silver, copper, and prime land for new Mexican consumers, particularly in the Yaqui valley.

Charlie rode hard and fast through the mountains. It felt too easy to pick up Wentworth's trail. The thought that he was walking into a trap occurred more than once. But his confrontation with Wentworth would be different. Charlie was finished running. He was now on the attack. Wentworth would fall, even if it meant killing every Federale soldier in Mexico. It would be to the death this time.

Charlie's personal arsenal was supplemented by a midnight shopping spree at Jose's general store. Two long-range Henry rifles, a double barreled sawed-off shotgun, a Winchester repeater, and of course, his hand-tooled revolvers. In his saddlebag, enough ammunition and dynamite to kill every Federale in Sonora three times over, with rounds left over to have target practice on Wentworth's head.

As the sun rose to its noon-day station in the sky, Charlie found himself riding along a dried riverbank bordered by jagged rocks on both sides. Heading east, horseprints from badly shod horses, probably a detachment of Federale cavalry. Going west, a single set of prints, made by a horse with a fresh set of shoes.

Charlie rode west. The trail narrowed, the hills around it soon becoming 300 foot cliffs. An ideal location where Wentworth could be hiding with a rifle. An interesting possibility, considering that Wentworth always had his subordinates do his killing for him. But the only thing predictable about Wentworth was his unpredictability. What was predictable was the trail, a clear imprint in the sand that could be followed by a blind man. Then the tracks disappeared. It was an old trick that Charlie had used many times. The easiest way to the hunted could trap an enraged or ignorant hunter. Or maybe this was to be the site for the final confrontation.

Through the neck-high weeds, Charlie saw a horse. A black thoroughbred-quarter horse cross; a Mexican Army brand on its rump. The tack was spotlessly clean, shining brightly in the sun.

The horse seemed to be standing at attention, waiting for its rider to return. A closer look revealed a Federale soldier on look-out duty relieving himself in the nearby bushes. His back was turned, his rank hidden.

Perhaps it was Wentworth, finally caught with his pants down. Perhaps not. Whoever it was would reveal Carlos' location most easily with a wounded arm or leg. Charlie's knowledge of anatomy told him where a bullet could cause the most pain, but the least amount of bleeding. Whoever this was, he needed him alive - especially if it was Wentworth.

Charlie took cover, aimed, then heard an old Yaqui tune from the bush. Into view of Charlie's sights came Diego, bringing a bagful of hand-picked berries to the horse.

Diego waved to Charlie, then kicked over the Federale, a 19 year old Lieutenant, stone dead, an unmistakable look of surprise on his peach-fuzzed face. Juan Garcia's rank was a gift from his uncle in the Mexican Army. His assignment in Yaqui Sonora was punishment from a politician who was to be his father-in-law. Diego didn't like killing teenage lieutenants, but if he didn't, they would become middle-aged majors or generals.

Diego rationalized most of his decisions on population arithmetic - and revenge. Diego's brothers died trying to escape a dispersal train, his wife and child massacred during Obregon's invasion of 1915. His father died of malaria and a broken spirit in a hacienda near the Guatemalan border. Diego had nothing to lose, making the decision of fighting the Mexicans or joining them a lot easier than it was for other Yaqui.

Diego secured his own private arsenal to the army saddle, an assortment of weaponry that included most everything except a machine-gun and artillery. Charlie approached.

"How's it going, Charlie?"

"Your horse?"

"Just got him."

"Where's Carlos?" Charlie asked Diego, demanding an answer.

"Down there, I think," Diego commented, pointing to a train on the flat moving at full speed. The cargo cars looked fuller than when Charlie had arrived, the guards better armed.

There was no better time than now for the final dispersal program. Diego knew that it would happen one day. The Federales would all capture the Yaqui villages one at a time. "Looks like we have a mutual problem," Diego commented to Charlie in the understated manner he used so often to hide his grief, anger, and fear.

"We have a mutual solution, too," Charlie countered. He commenced telling Diego the importance of killing Wentworth once and for all, relating stories about the industrial giant and demon he had not shared with anyone.

But Diego did not need much convincing. The bronco Yaqui was glad to finally have Charlie fighting with him. One vengeful man obsessed by a cause was dangerous. Two such souls were unstoppable.

An assault on the train while it was on the flat would be suicidal, and ineffective. But fifteen miles further south the tracks went through a steep, narrow, and very tortuous canyon. A train could be stopped there by a single boulder on the tracks. One man on the bottom could make his requests with a soft-spoken tone. The other man on the top could make sure those requests were carried out to the letter with a repeater rifle.

Charlie and Diego rode quickly through the high mountain passes. The horses felt their riders' sense of urgency and put out everything they had. There was ample time for Charlie and Diego to think. There was also ample time for them to argue about who would be on top of the canyon and who would negotiate on the bottom.

The argument was settled by an ambush. Twenty riders in pressed Federale uniforms with polished buttons sprang out of the cottonwoods and pointed their guns. It was a well planned ambush, made possible only by a man who knew those trails well, and these were Yaqui trails.

From out of the bushes emerged a Federale Colonel with a familiar face. Jose could still fit into his ten year-old Revolutionary uniform, all too proudly. The chestcoat was a bit snug, but the insignia fit him, all too well.

"So, Colonel Fernandez, you look handsome today," Diego commented, with a sarcastic tone so intrinsic to his nature. The boldness in his voice was the kind that was only possible in a man who had lived so dedicated a life that he was not afraid of death.

Charlie couldn't speak. He was angry at Wentworth for what he had done in Vicom. He was angrier at himself for arguing too loudly with Diego on the trail and giving away his position.

"General Espinoza and General Mori are a mile back, this way," Jose said to Diego. "Are you with us or against us?"

Diego remembered the two generals. Both mansos Yaqui, as "tame" as Jose. They were brave fighters, Diego remembered. Smart military tacticians, too. But stupid, when they actually expected to be granted the promise of "land and liberty" promised by Mexican politicians. Jose and Diego both wanted "land and liberty." As long as they fought each other, Obregon would emerge victorious. Jose knew this, and deep down, Diego did too. But that wouldn't stop the mansos and bronco Yaqui from killing each other over points of strategy.

Jose's men moved their guns close to Diego's head. Diego countered with silent defiance. "We have a train to stop," he said.

"So do we," Jose replied. He pointed down to another set of railroad tracks below. The train on it had barely five cars between the caboose and a French-made locomotive left over from the war against Emperor Maximillian. The cars were old, but had an elegant old-world design. They were heavily guarded by clean-shaven troops with repeater rifles, and by two machine guns strategically placed around the most elaborately-designed car. That car had red velvet curtains drawn over its windows.

Obregon's personal campaign train was well suited to take him wherever he wanted to go in style. Diego had once seen the campaign train, a portable fortress that he secretly admired, better defended than the Presidential Palace itself. He had never seen Jose's eyes so determined. So desperate. Not a word was spoken, but Diego knew that what Jose had in mind was so bold, so daring, that it would have to work. It had to.

Chapter 12

The events that occurred from this time onward were vague. The world would only know about the consequences of what happened, and almost nothing about the bizarre events that lead up to them. After all, Wentworth was involved in this, and anything he was tied up with somehow created confusion. And anything Charlie was tied up with somehow caused disaster.

It was the time for showdowns. For the Yaqui it would be a final confrontation with Obregon. For Charlie it would be, hopefully, a face to face with Wentworth, now one of Obregon's most prominent foreign financial supporters.

Mansos Yaqui Generals Espinoza and Mori already had things planned out. Their men were already looking over the secret ambush site Diego had chosen. But though the "where" was the same, the "how" would be very different.

A pile of rocks would be thrown onto the tracks below, giving the illusion of an avalanche. Espinoza and Mori's Yaqui warriors would pose as Federal soldiers and pretend to be clearing the tracks, requesting assistance in that endeavor from Obregon's elite guard. Jose's detachment would observe events from above and get the drop on Obregon's men at the appointed time or, if necessary, earlier. Diego and Charlie would be welcomed members of Jose's team, as long as they did not take matters into their own hands. If they did, they would be subdued by whatever means available. Espinoza and Mori would be in charge of dealing with Obregon, and they wanted him alive, for a very important and clandestine purpose.

The plan went according to schedule with no complications. No blood was spilled, no shots fired. Jose was given the honor of instructing the engineer to turn the train around and take it to Vicom. Diego was given the pleasure of shooting the engineer if he did not comply with the request. And, according to plan, the curtains on the Presidential car remained closed to the world outside.

President Obregon continued to write a speech about how he would oversee the carefully planned democratization of Mexico. The message boldly promised everything to everybody, the words carefully not committing anything to anyone. It was a self-absorbing process Obregon had gotten so good at that he often lost the ability to know when he was telling the truth and when he was lying.

Then, he heard a jolt. He looked outside the velvet curtain windows from behind his Victorian oak desk. The train was moving backward, the caboose overloaded with unarmed Federale soldiers held at gunpoint.

The site of a vigilante army of Yaqui head by Espinoza and Mori was frightening enough. But Obregon was to be taken by an even more vicious captor.

Charlie smashed through the window and pinned Obregon to the floor, smashing his face into it with a painful twist of his neck. It was not part of the Yaqui kidnapping plan, at least the one designed by Mori and Espinoza.

"Where's Wentworth?" Charlie demanded in a loud, uncontrolled scream. Before Obregon got a chance to breathe, Charlie whipped out his Bowie knife and put it to the President's throat. "Where's my son, Carlos!!!?"

"Wentworth isn't here. I don't know your son!!!" Obregon was too scared to lie, but Charlie was too angry to listen.

"You work for Wentworth. All you sons of bitches work for Wentworth. Where is he?!!!" Charlie's hands were drenched with sweat, the whites of his eyes beet red with rage. The whole Yaqui plan could be blown now, from the Yaqui perspective. Then, once again, fate intervened.

The door to Obregon's car opened. Behind it stood Generals Mori and Espinoza, and their most trusted comrades. Prominent amongst that group was Jose. Charlie would not let anyone have Obregon before he was finished with him.

Jose interceded with a calm voice of reason uniquely his own. "Charlie, give me the knife, please. We came to talk with President Obregon. We came to ask for peace. Peace, land and liberty."

Charlie had his own agenda. Land and liberty came after getting Carlos and extracting revenge on Wentworth. Obregon would confess at least one of his sins on his way to the afterlife. Charlie squeezed on Obregon's neck until his face turned blue, then pale. The mansos Yaqui stood back, knowing fully well that if they intervened, Charlie would snap Obregon's neck. The Yaqui watched, waited, and hoped that this improvisation would not ruin the big plan they intentionally kept from Charlie.

Obregon started to talk, in half grunts, then in half syllables. "Wentworth is...is...is...at...," Charlie's tortured soul could hear between the slurs and gasps.

Then, deliverance - for Obregon. Charlie was knocked over the head and fell to the floor. Standing beside him, his fist bruised by pounding on Charlie's hard head, Diego.

"This is a war for our liberation, not his," Diego said.

Jose dragged Charlie out. Obregon caught his breath with the desperation of a man who would sell his soul to avoid facing death with eyes wide open. Mori and Espinoza approached the President with a treaty. It was written in eloquent legalese, delivered with dignity and civility. Obregon sat at his desk and invited his guests to join him. He read. The Yaqui waited. Then they talked.

The train proceeded to the railhead in Vicom without incident. Anxious onlookers came from miles around. It was a hallmark in Mexican history, and a miracle to the Yaqui. They had kidnapped the President of Mexico, without firing a shot.

The negotiations inside Obregon's car went on for a few hours. Outside the train, it seemed like days, as the sun rose high in the sky and elevated temperature well above normal.

As a gesture of goodwill, Mori and Espinoza allowed the twenty captive Federales soldados to leave the train, but they preferred to stay on board. They were also allowed to keep their weapons, but only one round each. Twenty rounds against a thousand Yaqui soldiers. It was Diego's idea, intended to remind the Federales that they were conscripted soldiers, not passion-driven warriors.

Finally, a Federale messenger and an unarmed Yaqui escort left the Presidential car and walked toward the telegraph dispatch. Both were barely twenty years old. Both had smiles which would bring a long, productive, and happy life for their comrades and unborn children.

An unbridled expression of jubilation came from the onlookers. Expressions of joy resembling every real and imaginary creature in the Bacatetes. The Federales retreated back into the train, terrified. Their re-emergence was slow, but well worth the effort. The recruits popped up first, opening their minds, then hearts, to the most feared Indians in Mexico.

Charlie watched from outside the train, his head still throbbing. With him, Emma and John. In her instinctive way of knowing what Charlie needed to hear Emma commented, “I have a feeling that wherever Diane is, she’s happy today.”

They were words that were more formulated than felt. Still, Charlie was hard pressed to refute them, and he could not deny the sincerity with which they were delivered.

Emma assured Charlie that they would begin the search for Carlos the next day. John assured him of his help in the endeavor.

Charlie felt himself smiling. The comradeship offered by his fellow expatriates, and the optimism generated by the political events he was witnessing, melted his wall of anger and allowed hope to come to his battle-weary soul. He also found a way to put things into a bigger perspective, despite persistent attempts to hold on to his own.

Charlie looked into Diane’s eyes, and he saw the best of the past and the present. He was reminded of the old concept of universal compassion, which he so boldly championed in his Revolutionary days in New York, and which he so easily forgot in the wake of recent events here in Sonora. The Yaqui had lost wives and had children kidnapped, yet they chose to look toward the future, rather than dwell on the past. New friends can replace old ones, though no one is ever forgotten. That was the way things worked in nature, for both animals and man. Diane’s energy and efforts would never be lost. And if Carlos was still alive, he would be found.

Jose and Diego realized, perhaps for the first time, that they differed in matters of strategy, not principle. Finally - a “plan” where bronco and mansos Yaqui both got what they wanted - assimilation and autonomy.

The Federales began to realize the importance of the Yaqui spirit to the Mexican soul. Barely one in a hundred Mexicans didn’t have Aboriginal blood, and the purebred Yaqui were as Aboriginal as one could get in 1926 Mexico. Destroying the Yaqui would destroy a part of the collected Mexican soul. It was a passing feeling, but a new one for people who would be very influential one day.

There was much to be forgiven, or forgotten. Yaquis' and Mexicans' revenge had often been in excess of the offense taken, and tragically exerted on an innocent party, ensuring that the chain of retribution be extended. It would be up to the historians to paint the characters in the century-old Yaqui-Mexican war with the colors of their own choosing. But for that day, the Yaqui all envisioned themselves as guardians of the earth. Mexican settlement and political intervention in the Yaqui River valley and the Bacatetes would be by invitation only.

Obregon was at a loss for words when he emerged from his car, treaty in hand. He looked out at the silent crowd. He projected optimism with his bold presidential stride, but there was remorse in his defeated eyes. Many Yaqui felt victorious, then an emotion they expected least - pity.

Mori and Espinoza translated the legalese into Yaqui. But there were only three words that the crowd really listened to - "Peace, land, liberty." It was in the best interests of Mexican and Yaqui alike, and probably the wisest political decision of Obregon's career. A handshake, followed by a traditional Yaqui greeting between Obregon and the mansos generals, confirmed it.

The crowd burst into celebration. The Federales breathed a long awaited sigh of relief. Someone sang the anthem which inspired the overthrow of Diaz in the 1910 Revolution. Before the second stanza, everyone present had added their own voices in their language of preference.

The train whistle blew and churned its way toward the East, flowers thrown in its wake. Young women not spoken for waved to Federale recruits, with unspoken proposals for further contact that were mutually accepted. Then violins, flutes, drums and all manner of ordinary objects converted noise into music.

Forgiveness is an unexpected emotion. It sneaks up on a man when he lets go of anger and has reason gently thrust upon him. Charlie was overwhelmed with this feeling as he saw Obregon's train disappear into the horizon.

Diane was dead, but she did live a full life. And there was no proof that Wentworth's bullet killed her. Maybe Wentworth never left the United States, and the stories about the British industrialist expanding his empire to Sonora were imaginations of Charlie's tired mind. Carlos' body had not been found, and he could very well still be alive. Perhaps he was taken prisoner by the Federales and was going to be on his way back to Vicom on the next train, in the first wave of the inevitable return of dispersed Yaqui back to their homeland.

Time passed. Perhaps it was minutes. Perhaps it was hours. Perhaps days. No one was taking too much notice of passing of time that day. Yaqui history would not be written according to the Gregorian calendar, and the Yaqui concept of time used experience, not hours, as its unit measurement.

Then the real world and dream world melded, according to plan. Something no Federale could imagine, and no Yaqui expected.

A locomotive emerged from the distant Eastern horizon, pulling a long row of freight cars behind it. Obregon was indeed delivering on his promises, and quickly. It was in his political interest to restore to the Yaqui what they had lost during his administration as hastily as possible, and Obregon always did what was in his political interest.

A crowd gathered to greet the train, four thousand, some said, one in every five Yaqui in Sonora. All eyes gazed down the tracks, most particularly Charlie's. Eagerly awaited were the supplies promised in the treaty. Even more anticipated, the return of loved ones taken in the past dispersals, and the new one officially ordered by Obregon's disobedient subordinates.

The desert plays tricks with both time and space. It seemed like it took forever for the train to make the final turn into the railhead. Then a southeast wind rose up. The cars looked too tall, surreal. They seemed to slide on top of the hot desert air itself.

The train stopped outside of town, well in front of the crowd waiting to welcome it. Charlie galloped ahead of the mass of people approaching the train on foot. He soon would find Carlos telling a tall Yaqui tale to a gullible Federale soldier. Rumors came to him by telegraph-cryptic, but still understandable.

A rumor believed in grim reality, very easy to the faithful, and Charlie found himself in the ranks of believers.

Charlie's faith was rewarded as quickly as it was offered. From inside the caboose, Charlie heard music. An old nursery tune too familiar to be named, played on a scratchy phonograph, the melody given life by Carlos' voice. Then the door opened up, slightly. Then Carlos' laughter, very real and very loud, and shared by others. Charlie dismounted and rushed toward the door.

Charlie pushed it open. Carlos was alive. But, he was not well.

Carlos was sitting in a chair, rigidly at attention, as if posing for a photograph. He was dressed in a British Army uniform, identical to the one which Charlie wore during his sabbatical from life during World War I. But Carlos' rank was that of a General. His Commander in Chief - Wentworth, now standing behind him in a Private's Mexican Federale uniform.

Wentworth looked more surreal now that he ever had before. His complexion emanated the most gruesome hues of black, green, blue and white, all at once. Another phonograph, behind him, switched on. Beethoven's rendition of "God Save the King," the one Charlie used to love so much.

Introductions at the reunion took barely three seconds. Then Wentworth moved ahead, according to his timetable. "Give the order, please," he said calmly to Carlos.

"Fire," screamed Carlos, with a voice that Charlie recognized as his own when he was a youth.

Charlie look outside. Well-armed Federale troops jumped out of the train and began to shoot on the crowd of Yaqui who had converged on the train. The troops were a mixture of infantry and cavalry, armed to the teeth, with back up from four machine guns.

Charlie looked back toward Wentworth, fully prepared to pay whatever price was required to stop the killing. But Wentworth and Carlos were gone. All that remained was the record player and Charlie's old medals from his days in the Great War. Charlie threw the phonograph outside in frustration. The record broke, but Charlie could still hear the music echoing in his mind at full volume.

Diego and Jose did what they could to organize the Yaqui men into a fighting unit. John and Emma helped in the evacuation of the women and children.

Charlie jumped a cavalry officer and stole his horse. He disarmed several infantrymen and knocked two more officers from their horses. But as long as the Federales had control of the machine guns, they would have control of the "battle."

Those guns could fire twenty rounds a second, but they had to be reloaded. Charlie eyed one Federale machine gun nest, near the end of its belt. In front of it lay thirty dead Yaqui, shock frozen on their stone-dead faces. Charlie was determined to even the score.

Charlie assessed his options. He had only four bullets left in his revolver, and ten times that many Federales between him and the machine gun. He would have to move quickly, and have some help. Suddenly, assistance came in the form of a familiar voice.

"I'll cover ya," John yelled out. He picked up a repeater rifle, instantly finding in himself the skill and courage to use it effectively. Charlie galloped toward the machine gun nest, oblivious to the shots that penetrated into his left thigh and right arm. He continued on, unimpeded.

The Federales valued life, and realized that Charlie didn't, so they retreated. Charlie shot the two infantrymen guarding the nest on top of the train, then dismounted and climbed up to it. Only one thing now stood in his way, a Federale sergeant reloading the gun.

Charlie pointed his revolver at the sergeant's head and cocked it. The Federale continued in his duty of loading the gun, fully realizing the consequences of displaying valor under fire.

Once again, time slowed down for Charlie, while the rest of the world around him moved at a frenzied spiral. He ordered the sergeant to move aside, a request that went unheeded. Then Charlie made his biggest mistake.

He looked into the sergeant's eyes. They were the eyes of a soldier who was honoring his pledge to the Republic of Mexico, not a butcher of defenseless Indians. It was the austere face of duty which Charlie had seen so often in the Great War, and which served so well to perpetuate that conflict.

Charlie warned him again, but the sergeant did what he had to do, as did Charlie. He fired a bullet straight into the sergeant's skull.

Then, he had an agonizing realization. Charlie realized that he somehow enjoyed the killing. He also realized that he always had enjoyed killing. Destruction was intrinsic to Charlie's nature, and it was only by the saving grace of some Divine Power that it could be kept under control or directed into useful pursuits.

The heat of battle gives you time to see different aspects of your internal pathology. It does not afford you the time to treat it. Charlie came back to the time frame of the massacre. He turned the Gatling gun around, and sprayed bullets at any Federale in sight like a rabid lunatic. It didn't matter if they were approaching him, threatening the Yaqui, running away, or surrendering. In front of him, an unending stream of death.

Chaos and tragedy ruled the day.

John's corpse was spread out on the ground in several pieces. Emma's body lay face down in the dirt, her pale hand still holding on to the bodies of the two Yaqui children she was trying to protect. Jose's chest was penetrated by a sword, which belonged to a Federale cavalry officer who was once a comrade-in-arms in the art of liberation. Both lay dead on the blood-soaked ground, confusion in their lifeless eyes.

Diego took what remained of the Yaqui up into the mountains, trying to keep them ahead of the advancing Federale troops. He was the most valuable person the Yaqui had to lead them in the kind of war which lay ahead.

Meanwhile, Charlie kept firing as many bullets as he could, until he was finally clubbed with a rifle butt. He fell to the ground, unconscious but still alive. If he had been killed, it would have been a blessing. But Wentworth was in control now, and he was determined that Charlie would pay for his transgressions, in a very big way.

Chapter 13

There's nothing more dangerous than a man with nothing to lose. There's also nothing more tragic.

Charlie found himself in a jail cell, his head pounding, his ankles and wrists in chains. Imprisonment for participation in unsanctioned political activities was nothing new to Charlie. Having no one on the outside to fight for was.

Charlie sang aloud an American cowboy song which he had picked up in West Texas before all the revolutions started. "Big Sky Dreamer" was never a big hit in New York, but it held a special place for drifters like Charlie. It helped him remember times in the past when dreams could be enjoyed, but did not have to be tested.

Drunk with disillusionment, Charlie bellowed out the tune with discordant notes, changing keys several times with each verse. The guards neither understood the words to the song, nor the emotions behind them. But it kept the Gringo prisoner occupied. It also kept the other inmates scared to death. Both suited the authorities in charge.

The Yaqui were the closest family Charlie had, but he had a way of bringing death to those closest to him. Maybe it was now time for Charlie to consider paying back the debt which Wentworth was so cleverly trying to extract from him.

With that thought, Charlie heard a steady cadence of bootheels in the hallway. The procession was led by a Federale captain. Captain Rivera lost two brothers in the "police action" in Vicom. He desperately wanted revenge, but his political office demanded that it be done within the framework of the law.

Charlie was an American, and a famous one at that. The American government could be a generous friend, or a merciless enemy. Charlie's case had to be handled swiftly, tactfully, and with the utmost secrecy.

"In accordance with Mexican law, you are entitled to a trial," Rivera related to Charlie in perfect English and dispassionate military civility. "You go in front of the judge in an hour."

Charlie persisted in ignoring the captain. His singing got even louder and more discordant. Rivera firmly threw a tan suit and white shirt into Charlie's cell. "It would be better if you looked presentable," he continued.

Charlie stopped singing. The clothes smelled all too familiar, the odor of blood and urine from the former owners still as strong as ever. He looked up at the Captain. "Fuck you," he said in a calm voice, after which he began to sing again, loud and crazy. Crazier than any other prisoner in the history of the facility.

Rivera's eyes burned with rage. He nodded. The guards opened the cell door. Charlie smiled.

The guards strapped Charlie against the wall, arms spread and legs tied together. A crucifixion stance, Charlie thought. A Christian death for a Judas goat. But after glory comes pain, and there would be pain. Death by the hand of another, rather than yourself, still allowed you entry into Christian Paradise, and part of Charlie was still Christian.

Rivera rose up the ranks more for his horsemanship than his military wisdom. His cruelty in the field was legendary. If driven to it, Rivera could skin a man alive, remove half his visceral organs, and still keep him alive enough to beg for the mercy of death. He never posted sentries, preferring to use the heads of his enemies to delineate the camp perimeters. Rivera never went anywhere without his aristocratic bearing, his father's watch, and his bullwhip.

Rivera cracked the custom-made whip firmly near Charlie, taking out a chunk of plaster from the wall from a predesignated spot. The next blow would inevitably remove a larger portion of Charlie's flesh, but the once optimistic expatriate did not care.

Rivera prepared to demand personal satisfaction, despite the political consequences.

Charlie sang a final verse of "Big Sky Dreamer." He closed his eyes and clenched his fist. He offered a silent prayer to a God who he hoped was still alive, and listening. He asked for a quick delivery from the misery of life - and he got it.

"Let him down," Charlie heard in an English accent - all too familiar. Wentworth walked into the cell, wearing a brown suit with a matching cape, a riding crop in his right hand. "I am his lawyer."

Wentworth gave the Captain a document written in red ink. "You have been ordered to remand him into my custody," he explained calmly.

Charlie protested, but to no avail. Death by a Federale whip would undoubtedly be more merciful and honorable than whatever Wentworth had in mind. But Wentworth was persuasive, as always, and no one - not even Captain Rivera the infamous - dared to disobey.

The Federales marched down the hall, leaving Charlie chained to the cell wall. Wentworth talked in casual pleasantries, Charlie remained silent.

Wentworth finally stopped talking. He turned to Charlie, direct, succinct. "Charlie, we have to settle this matter once and for all. It has gone on too long, for both of us." The chains around Charlie's wrists and ankles broke apart. Charlie noticed the cell door open, giving way to the sunlight of the outside world. There was a sense Charlie's horse waited outside the gates, saddled and ready to go.

Wentworth extended his hand toward the three-foot thick concrete wall behind Charlie and bowed slightly. "After you," he uttered with gentlemanly respect, requesting Charlie to walk into the wall. Appearing on the wall - a black, then white door, fading into, then out of Charlie's delirious mind.

"Follow me, please," Wentworth instructed Charlie. With that the English industrialist walked through the concrete wall, clearly demonstrating his ability to effortlessly master time and space.

Charlie remained. An escape out of the cell down the hallway would be safer, a continuation of the cat and mouse game the fugitive-revolutionary had been well accustomed to. But Wentworth was right. It was time to settle things, once and for all.

As that realization came to Charlie's mind, he could hear Wentworth's voice coming from the other side of the wall, inviting him to cross over. Charlie slowly extended his hand toward the wall. It became absorbed into it. He pulled it out, and found that it was still intact. He then took a firm step into the wall with his right foot, then an even bolder stride with his left.

Charlie emerged on the other side of the wall in a Cathedral. Paintings of the Creation in the style of Michelangelo on the ceiling. Marble columns with likenesses of the Saints. The walls were covered with stained glass reliefs which told the story of Christ's birth, life, death and resurrection in multicolored images more intense than any written account of these events. But the sacred altar was gone, its place occupied by two coffins made of finely crafted cedarwood, gold handles on their sides.

And, of course, there was Wentworth. His suit had turned from brown to red, his riding crop transformed into a pitchfork, with two sharp horns emerging from his head, leaving no doubt about his demonic identity. This particular "look" was chosen for Charlie. Though reason taught Charlie that demonic creatures were only found in storybook legends, the genius-revolutionary still couldn't shake the belief that Satan was as real as God, Jesus, or even the huya aniya.

Charlie noticed something else. The wounds incurred during the fighting in Vicom and the beatings in jail were gone.

Wentworth smiled. He then put his arm into and out of the "entrance" wall to the cathedral several times. "Ah, yes, theatrics," Wentworth commented. "They are amazing. I believe the peasants here call them miracles. But I do still enjoy them...so do you."

Charlie reflected on the truth of that remark. He never could accept the way things were, even if they were good. The political revolutions defied the laws of social restraint. The science experiments dared to understand, then change nature, and his practice of medicine was a rebellion against death. Whether these obsessions were a vice, virtue, or an obligation was still in question.

As Charlie pondered these internal issues, Wentworth took him for a tour around the Cathedral to discuss the business at hand. This time, nothing would be inferred. Everything would be spelled out, all too clearly.

Wentworth's tone was cordial and occasionally pleasant. Charlie remained defiant.

"I was young, I was desperate," Charlie stated, in defense of Wentworth's unspoken list of accusations.

"And you prayed for wizardry, Charlie."

"I was a kid. I prayed for superior intelligence. The gift of genius and the ability to use it. From anyone who could give it to me. I wanted that intelligence so that I could take away your power."

Wentworth let out a condescending laugh that echoed through the Cathedral. It pounded into every bone of Charlie's body. "Ah, yes. My 'power'," Wentworth commented.

Behind him was a stained glass representation of the Temptation of Christ by Satan in the desert, made by a well-intended artist who understood neither the compassion of Christ nor the true source of the Temptation. He continued, glancing at the inaccuracies of his representation of the glass. "I am the 'ruler of evil'. The 'prince of darkness'. You know it is your fear that gives me power. And it is your ignorance which gives me form. And, my dear Charlie, you humans have no shortage of either fear or ignorance."

Wentworth proceeded to a hand-carved walnut table. On it was a gold-plated goblet, brightly reflecting the candles that all emitted flames ice-cold to the touch. The air in the Cathedral turned hotter and Charlie felt a parchness in his throat, a thirst more painful than anything he had experienced in the Sonoran or Texan desert.

Wentworth dipped the goblet into a font of holy water and offered Charlie a drink. Charlie reached his hand out. Wentworth smiled as Charlie brought the cooling water closer to his lips. Then, a turn of events. Something in Charlie would not let him surrender, even though the scoreboard showed game over, and score of infinity to nothing against him. Charlie pushed the goblet aside. It broke on the floor, its water turned into fire that encircled Charlie, then miraculously stopped.

After a well-timed delay, Wentworth smiled. He helped himself to another cup of holy water, emitting a loud expression of his quenched thirst. He then moved on, allowing Charlie to follow at his own pace.

"Then again, there is a side of your species which enjoys inflicting suffering on others - or yourself," Wentworth continued. Murals displaying the crucifixion in graphic detail reinforced his claim. "Sadism and masochism. You are fascinated with them both...I did NOT give you these things." He punctuated his remarks with a penetrating stare. Behind him, a painting of peasants caught between colorfully-drawn demons and an expressionless, pale Madonna. "It is still interesting that my most obedient slaves are those who look at me with one eye opened with fascination, and the other eye covered with the blindfold of 'goodness'."

Charlie had heard enough metaphors and metaphysical accusations. He demanded to talk business. But Wentworth persisted, reminding Charlie of the futility of resisting him, and the childishness of his vision of the universe.

Charlie had lost his belief in a lot over the years, but he never lost his belief in the nobility of the human spirit and its connection to rugged individualism. "We're strong enough to fight you," Charlie stated firmly, in the face of Wentworth's continued taunting.

"Who is 'we'?" inquired Wentworth in a condescending tone. "Do you mean humanity? Do you think that humanity is strong enough to fight me AND my brother, God? He is in charge of dispersing happiness. I am in charge of dispersing suffering. Even we can't change that. What makes you think that you, or any other moral creature on earth, can change that?"

"Energy created can't be destroyed," Charlie rebutted, hoping that science could be used against injustice. "Good intentions, sincerity, dedication are the most powerful forms of energy."

Wentworth countered with a loud laugh. "Charlie, if you believed that, we would not be having this conversation at all." The chill that penetrated Charlie's sweat-soaked body supported Wentworth's claim all too tragically.

Wentworth walked on to the coffins at the front of the Cathedral. Charlie followed. Wentworth's tone turned abruptly businesslike. "There are no cheap theatrics here, Charlie."

He pushed the coffins upright, then opened them with a crowbar. What lay inside was the most frightening part of the tour.

In the first coffin, Emma's body. Her hair was meticulously groomed, her dress from the finest Parisian designers. No undertaker or curator could have done a better job in giving the appearance of life to a dead body. "One of my 'experiments' in breeding," Wentworth commented dispassionately.

Charlie knew Wentworth's real identity since World War I, though he continuously tried to deny it. But he could never deny the humanity in Wentworth's daughter. Emma's humanity was something Charlie could never understand, but he was always attracted to it. No sight could have horrified him more - so he thought.

Wentworth opened the second coffin. Carlos' corpse was preserved in the manner of an English gentlemen, authoritative austerity frozen into his face. Wentworth reminded Charlie that Carlos was the product of his own breeding experiments with mortals.

Charlie rushed to the corpses, but could not bring himself to touch them.

"They look almost lifelike. But I can do better," Wentworth commented.

He snapped his fingers. Emma and Carlos' eyes looked around the room. Their bodies remained dead, trapping their minds in an iron-clad prison of cold flesh. Their faces showed utter confusion and immeasurable pain..

"Bring them back!!! All the way back!!!" Charlie protested loudly, with a desperation that he rarely showed to anyone.

Wentworth remained calm, and once again used logic to distort reason. "Raise the dead? If I do it, that would be witchcraft. Perhaps you could do it, but that would be blasphemy. Only the Christ can raise the dead, you know. And you, Charlie, are not the Christ. You never were the Christ. And you never will be."

Charlie desperately tried to shake Emma and Carlos out of the world of the living dead. He breathed into their clammy mouths, hoping that he could blow life into their cold bodies.

"It can't be done, Charlie," Wentworth said. "Your new-found God of Sincerity is powerful enough to change the rules. The rules we need to prevent our universe from falling apart."

Charlie continued, defiantly. He embraced the torsos made stiff by rigor mortis, hoping to resurrect these two very special people. "Come on, Goddamit. Come on!!!" he screamed repeatedly, as both a command and a prayer.

Finally, Emma and Carlos came to life, then sat up. They looked at their surroundings and their apparel in bewilderment. Then, at Charlie, in the hope that he could give them an explanation.

Wentworth provided a smattering of applause. "Very good, Charlie. I am impressed," he said in all truthfulness. After all, sincerity was a 'trick' that Charlie learned on his own.

But no matter how proud Wentworth was of Charlie, he could not let him go. It was time for the games to continue, and there would be only one victor in this final round.

Chapter 14

Charlie, Emma and Carlos enjoyed a three-way embrace in the Cathedral, tears of joy for each other, thanks to whatever Entity made the reunion possible.

But the reunion was brief, and the battle proceeded according to schedule. The trio was transported across time and space once again to a dry desert hill, somewhere in the Middle East. Charlie was nailed to a large cross. Blood poured out of his palms and feet, yet he felt no pain. Behind him, Emma and Carlos were naked, tied to smaller crosses with barbed wire. The hot sun had dehydrated their throats and spirits, and their screams of pain dulled to moans of agony.

Charlie looked away. Another dimension of the horror. A crowd of faceless onlookers garbed in a variety of historical apparel applauded him, mad with admiration.

Wentworth approached Charlie, clad as a Roman Centurion. "Illusion or reality, Charlie. Either way, you do have to do business with me."

Charlie looked behind him and saw a multitude of old friends, dying on what seemed to be an unending row of crosses. Diane, John, Jose, and numerous others who had fallen in the battle which, in one way or the other, involved Charlie. If Charlie had not come to the Yaqui valley, they would still be alive, he thought. Wentworth read his thoughts immediately and affirmed that belief with a smile, and then a laugh.

The applause of the crowd got louder. Moans from behind Charlie turned into deafening screams. Wentworth continued, with an eagerness of a demented carnival M.C. on a July 4th picnic. "A contest would be fun. Let's have some fun, Charlie, whatdoyasay, Charlie?"

Wentworth raised his hands. The crowd went into a wild frenzy. Charlie looked at Wentworth's smiling face and spit into it.

The crowd turned abruptly silent, and Wentworth wiped the saliva from his eyes and mouth. He looked up at Charlie with the most vengeful of stares, projecting an intensity which even Charlie had not seen before. That stare was made all the more fearful by his announcing to the crowd, in a cheering tone through gritted teeth, "Charlie said yes. He said yes."

The crowd burst out into uncontrolled jubilation at the news. The battlefield changed once again. The final skirmish in a long, bloody war.

The chosen arena was common ground. Charlie found himself on the plateau of a desert mountain which peaked above all those around it. It was arid, windblown and rocky. The cracks in the ground had been baked in by the sun and frozen in place by the cold night air. The arena was bordered with patches of brown prairie grass and low lying cactus.

Charlie was clad in a fringed buckskin shirt and knee-high leather moccasins. His trousers were light denim, and fit snugly around his legs. Beside him was a horse of good temperament, and a conformation that seemed conducive for maneuverability on uneven terrain. Behind Charlie were several lances stuck into the ground in a row, ready for use.

Wentworth approached the steep plateau from the opposite side. He rode up the steep slope mounted on a 17-hand black quarterhorse-thoroughbred, with large feet that belonged more appropriately to a draft horse. He was clad in black from head to toe. His long cape was wrapped around his chest, affording him the element of surprise as to what was under it.

"There are no audiences here, Charlie," Wentworth announced, as he took his spot for the joust. "The rules are simple. You live, you win. I live, you lose."

Wentworth pulled a shiny saber out of his cape. Charlie assessed the variety of lances provided him. They represented an assortment of armaments, which ranged from Aboriginal spears to the modern lances used so effectively by the British in the Crimean War.

Charlie chose a Lakota spear. Its shaft was made of wood, but it could be maneuvered easily and thrown with deadly accuracy if required. He mounted his horse and stared defiantly into Wentworth's eyes.

Wentworth dug his spurs into his horse's flank and rushed on toward Charlie at a lope. Charlie nudged his horse on with his calves and punctuated the gesture with a flick of the reins on his rump. Wentworth broke into a gallop. Charlie did the same.

Wentworth extended his sword straight ahead. Charlie countered with an extension of his spear. When skillfully wielded, the double-edged saber could cut off a man's arm. If properly held, the spear could penetrate through an opponent's chest.

The two horsemen drew targets on each other with their minds, focusing their weapons on their mark. It was an even match, physically. But Charlie made the mistake of bringing fear to the contest, disguised as caution. As the charge proceeded, Charlie let fear out of its box, along with its first cousin, guilt. Those thoughts were active participants in Charlie's mind for no more than a second, but a second was all that Wentworth needed.

Wentworth emerged from the first bout on his horse, his sword and his torso intact. Charlie was on the ground, lance broken, its pieces dropping into a crevice too narrow and deep for retrieval.

Wentworth stood his ground on the other side of the field, then started his lope toward Charlie. Charlie mounted his horse, then pulled out another lance from the ground. A lightweight model which had been used by Maximillian's army barely fifty years ago in this country.

This round, Charlie was not going to lose. The lance he had chosen had a firm metal shaft and a razor-sharp tip. He was determined that its tempered steel would penetrate through whatever armor Wentworth had under his cloak, and do him in once and for all. Steel would kill the demon who protected the Industrial Revolution. Fire would be used to kill the devil.

Charlie prodded his horse into a hand gallop. Wentworth's horse broke its stride, then slowed down to a trot with a prominent head nod, indicative of a stone bruise.

Finally, Charlie's chance. He kicked his horse into a flat out gallop and stood tall in the saddle, the lance firmly aimed at Wentworth's chest. He couldn't miss. Charlie was approaching too fast to be stopped by any weapon with which he was familiar. Wentworth had elected to play this game by human rules. And it looked like Charlie was going to finally win it.

Then, a very human tool was used against Charlie. Wentworth put up a shield in the form of a mirror. Time slowed down as Charlie saw his reflection in it. The image was bloody, awful and distorted. The sight of Charlie's ugliest faces in that mirror gave power to his most self-destructive emotions.

Wentworth held his ground and moved the mirror so that it would shine light into Charlie's horse's eyes. The steed reared up, dropped its rider on the ground, and ran off into the valley below the plateau at a full gallop.

"Strike two," Wentworth commented as he circled around Charlie. Wentworth's horse had miraculously overcome the stone bruise. Either that, or its rider was forceful enough to make the animal ignore the pain. In any case, the ominous messenger of death took his spot at the far end of the plateau. Charlie ran to his collection of armaments laid out for his use. Perhaps he could still fight Wentworth on foot. He had to.

Wentworth began his charge. The brim of his hat covered his face. The shadow of the afternoon sun made it look like a deep hole.

Charlie grabbed another lance, but they were all stuck into the ground. No amount of force was going to get them out. "Time to die, Charlie," Wentworth shouted in an echoing voice, as he approached Charlie at a flat out gallop.

There was nowhere to run. Behind Charlie was a thousand foot drop into a dried-up river bed. Ahead was something even more deadly. Wentworth's face took on bizarre proportions and a frightening constellation of archetypal images. First it was that of a black knight, from the storybooks Charlie was frightened of as a child. Then the images took on the form of demons from Charlie's older years. Good alternated with evil in a frightening constellation of images under Wentworth's forehead. Faces of people representing the best intentions of Heaven, and the cruelest demands of hell, took turns in showing themselves, adding their voices progressively to a common request, "Die, Charlie. Die."

No one in Charlie's life or imagination seemed to be excluded from the company of the ghostly chorus. The faces of the young scottish Lieutenant, the defiant Texas prospector, the recently slain John Smith, and even Diane herself commanded Charlie to pay for his sins. The tool was put into Charlie's own hand. He looked downward and saw a dagger in it. To his left an open grave materialized, his name chiseled on the tombstone in gold, and an American flag attached just above the salutation to the famous hero of the Great War.

Charlie knew these were only images, but fear was severing the few threads still linking his mind and his spirit. Death by his own hand was very inviting, and it would not be the first time that a warrior chose such a fate in the face of a charge by an insurmountable adversary. To make such an exit more attractive and logical, the constants of time and space became less constant than ever. Wentworth's horse advanced at a slower pace, its image becoming progressively larger and more frightening.

Charlie tried to hold on to any solid footing he could find, while the earth shook beneath his feet. But he was alone, and saw one way out. The easiest defense against a charging army is a bullet delivered into your own brain, and the dagger was sharp enough to work quickly. Still, something inside Charlie compelled him to hold on. He defiantly threw the dagger to the ground. The grave with his name on it disappeared.

Then there was a cloud of dust coming between Charlie and Wentworth's steed. Laying in front of Charlie's feet was an O'Brien anti-tank "rifle" with shells that could penetrate two inch armor, preloaded with ten rounds in mint condition.

The bearer of the gift appeared. The Shaman who Charlie saw in his nightmares in Texas, and then in his pilgrimage across the Bacatete mountains. The visitor from the huya aniya looked at Charlie with weary eyes. He had clearly come a long way to be here.

"I can beat him with this," Charlie said with enthusiasm, as he prepared to use the OB128 anti-tank special against his life-long adversary. "I can beat him with this," he repeated with gratitude, appended by the Yaqui word for that sentiment.

The Shaman cracked a sorrowful smile, nodded his head, and then turned around to become absorbed into the land once again.

"No," Charlie screamed abruptly. The Shaman turned around and looked at Charlie, waiting for him to make the next move.

"I can beat him with this," Charlie commented, as he looked down at the OB128 in his hand. He threw the weapon away, letting it fall down the steep cliffs isolating the sagebrush arena from the desert around it. He held up a clenched fist.

"I CAN beat him with that rifle, but I SHOULD beat him with this fist." The Shaman smiled warmly, a happy smile which he seldom showed or felt. He spoke a few encouraging words in Yaqui to Charlie, praising his decision to fight the devil with his heart, rather than with his trickery. Charlie understood the words very well, despite the fact that he had never heard them before.

The Shaman faded into the desert, fully realizing that Charlie's fate was now completely in his own hands. Neither the angels of Heaven nor the huya aniya could guarantee anything now. Charlie knew this, too, as the image of his guide vanished before his eyes.

The dust cloud in front of Charlie cleared up. Wentworth could see Charlie now, and charged at a flat out gallop. Wentworth's face was now completely taken over by a distorted image of demons, all screaming "time to die, Charlie," in deadly harmony. The sentiments were backed up by a deadly lance, eight razor-sharp blades extending out from its tip. Each of those blades was ear-marked for Charlie, and the wielder of that weapon was fully capable of hitting his mark this time.

Wentworth approached closer and closer, but Charlie stood firm, repeating "no more, no more," with the concentration of a Buddhist yoga and the determination of a zealous religious martyr. The Texan defenders of the Alamo were no less determined than Charlie. But, then again, such determination did not stop General Santa Anna from massacring those gallant heroes to the last man with a single assault.

Time slowed down again as Charlie stood his ground with a clenched fist. Then, in an intense moment which had been prayed for and dreaded since his youth, Charlie felt Wentworth's lance go through his chest. The pain was excruciating. The chorus of demons continued to haunt him, repeating in a disharmonious echo, "Time to die, Charlie. Time to die."

"No," Charlie commanded. "No more. No more." He gathered the strength that he could and climbed up the lance to choke the life out of Wentworth with his bare hands. The lance tore Charlie's organs apart. So did the voices. Charlie continued. The pain reached levels so high that he became numb to everything except the final mission. He reached out his bloody hand to Wentworth's head and grabbed his throat. He held onto the neck of a demon which displayed the most frightening representations of good and evil. All the biblical characters were there, the Old Testament God of fire and brimstone and the devil leading the chant. “Die, Charlie. Die,” they repeated in a deafening screech.

“No,” Charlie replied calmly. He let go of the monster’s throat and backed down. Then he pulled the lance out of his body, and glanced up at the demon creature. “YOU die. We don’t need you anymore.”

Charlie got up and pushed the creature off the horse. What fell to the ground was Wentworth’s hat, his cape, and the pitch-black outfit which he wore to the contest. Wentworth’s body disappeared in a cloud of smoke, quickly blown away by the desert winds. Charlie breathed a long awaited sigh of relief. He fainted to the ground with exhaustion, and then became unconscious.

Chapter 15

Charlie woke up in a time and space a long way from the windblown plateau. He was not sure what happened there, but something did. It must have. The dream felt too real to be an illusion.

There was no more fight left in Charlie. If a victory had really been won, he was too tired to feel the satisfaction of a job well done. If more work lay ahead of him, he was too exhausted to take up the challenge. Charlie opened his eyes slowly. Above him were several silhouettes. Human silhouettes, speaking human voices. Each said his name in turn and then remained silent, watching and waiting.

Charlie's eyes focused. Emma and Diego were alive but tired, very tired. Behind them was the harmonic chaos of Diane's clinic in the Bacatetes. The once plentiful medical supplies were exhausted, the beds full. Yaqui who could be moved were being evacuated. Those who could not were sharpening knives and arrowheads.

"Welcome back, Charlie," Diego said, with a smile he shared so seldomly with others. The smile was brief, interrupted by a reconnaissance band of Yaqui horsemen.

Emma removed a wet sponge from Charlie's forehead. There was a special look in her eye, one of satisfaction, exhaustion, and confidence. The once spoiled daughter of the most powerful industrialist in Europe had been carrying out medical duties with the instinct of a seasoned professional. It seemed appropriate that Emma would inherit this clinic. It also seemed appropriate that she would inherit Diane's place in Charlie's heart.

Charlie looked at himself in the mirror. His face was recognizable enough, but not the surgical greens he was wearing, nor the operating mask tied around his neck.

"Your surgery and our medicine - they saved many lives," Diego said, by way of explanation. "Thank you," he continued. He had not spoken those two words to a Gringo in a long time. Indeed, he had not uttered that sentiment to most anyone for as long as he could remember.

As Diego answered an urgent summons from the band of horsemen outside, Charlie stuttered incomprehensibly.

"Who, where, what?" was all that came out of his parched mouth. "Shhh . . .," Emma said in a soothing tone, which Charlie finally felt able to accept.

Diego came back in, armed with as much weaponry as his body could carry. "We have to leave now. Obregon's men will be back."

"Where will you go?" asked Charlie.

"The mountains. They'll give us shelter, and comfort. As soon as the others can be moved, bring them to the ravine north of here. You know the place."

"I'll see that they get there."

"And when they do, YOU keep riding north. Back to Texas, and then New York. Someone has to tell the world what happened here."

"They'll be told," Charlie pledged.

Diego got on his horse and prepared to ride off to a guerrilla war that looked like it would be one of the fiercest ever waged by him. Obregon had an unlimited supply of infantry and cavalry. He also had several new airplanes, equipped with bombs and mercenary pilots who would drop them wherever they were requested to. But the Yaqui had the advantage. As long as one Yaqui survived Obregon's reprisals, there would still be a Yaqui nation. And the Yaqui were survivors.

Charlie got up from bed, against Emma's medical orders and personal request. He was very weak but insisted on seeing Diego off - and seeing what had happened to this unnamed village hideout. Charlie stumbled to the door and fell down. A hand reached out to help him up.

"I'm okay. I can get up by myself," Charlie protested.

The hand remained out. Charlie looked up. Carlos had a slight cut on his forehead, but was otherwise fine. The boy had seen much tragedy that week. But he still chose to dwell upon the joy of life, rather than its miseries.

Charlie embraced Carlos with as much force as he could, nearly crushing the boy's chest. Carlos was confused as to why Charlie was displaying such an unusual feeling of affection. The boy knew nothing about Charlie's duel with Wentworth during his sabbatical from worldly reality. As far as Carlos knew, he was kidnapped by the Federales, held in a detention cell, liberated by one of Diego's guerrilla groups after the massacre at Vicom, and then dropped off at this hide-out village.

Emma came out of the hospital looking for Charlie. She smiled as she saw Charlie and Carlos finally united as father and son, friend and comrade, against the western sky. As her eyes swept the horizon, she gasped in disbelief. Approaching at a walk from the east was Wentworth.

Charlie pulled Carlos behind him and held on to him for dear life. Emma latched onto Charlie's arm as she fearfully eyed the arrival of her father.

Wentworth's walk was feeble, his head bowed. His riding boots were reduced to tattered leather sandals by the rocks, sagebrush and cactus. He had walked a long distance from his world to Charlie's in a very short time.

As Wentworth approached the trio of terror-stricken souls, he raised his head slightly. His face was very human. The wrinkles in his sunbaked face were deep enough to absorb a hundred miles of blood, sweat and tears. In his eyes was a repentance that was even deeper.

Wentworth seemed lost amidst the Yaqui evacuation, and as vulnerable as a child, orphaned from both family and friends and desperately needing them both. Charlie commanded Emma and Carlos to remain behind. He approached slowly.

"What do you want?" Charlie screamed at his life-long adversary. "We had a deal. I beat you! I won, and you lost!"

Wentworth bowed his head and remained silent. Charlie yelled louder. "What do you want, Goddamnit? What the hell do you want???!!!"

"Forgiveness."

Wentworth's request was simple and sincere. But in all the time Charlie knew Wentworth, the Englishman was hardly simple, and never sincere.

He presented Charlie with a jar wrapped in old newspaper held together by strands of second-hand yellow and blue ribbons, Emma's favorite colors.

Emma's apprehension escalated to fear, then terror.

"Charlie. What's going on?!" she screamed from a safe distance.

Wentworth could sensee in Emma's voice the love she had for Charlie, and the fear she felt towards himself.

"A wedding gift . . . I brought a wedding gift," Wentworth yelled out, loud enough for his daughter to hear.

Charlie opened the "gift," prepared to reject it on the spot once its identity was known. But its identity was something Charlie would have never expected.

It was a simple jar, containing a piece of brain tissue fixed in formalin.

"For twenty-seven years, I was carrying this tumor in my head. I had it removed recently." Wentworth took off his hat, revealing a shaved area on his scalp, with mild edema around the suture lines.

Wentworth put his hat back on and continued, "It made me quite mad for twenty-seven years, I am told. It was your cryostatic technology and reconstructive surgical techniques that made the operation possible. Thank you."

Charlie asked a few more questions regarding the surgery and the machinery used to do it. It all checked out. And the story was too incredible not to believe. A strange story to an educated mind. A special story to an enlightened one, where dreams and reality merge into a wondrous phenomenon called life. Parallel universes, working in harmony, made sense from a scientific, philosophical and religious perspective. Einstein's theory of relativity said that time was an illusion, and that each of us live in a universe which we define by what we see. What we see is determined by the speed of light, and since we are all at different positions in space, light from distant sources reaches all of us at different times. What our mortal eyes see as "reality" is a bombardment of light which reflects past events. Yet, Einstein also knew that while we all see different images of the universe we can, and must, feel the presence of everyone around us. Thus, our two-dimensional vision makes us live in our own unique "illusion," yet our hearts enable us to connect to our fellow beings.

The Yaqui elders knew the differences between the world of forms and the so-called "dream" world. The wonders of nature and the spirit of the earth, the huya aniya, connected them.

The East Indian Vedas spoke of "maya" as the illusion of life in the "gross plane," yet the sacred Gita stressed the importance of not abandoning one's responsibilities in that realm.

By his own hand, Charlie had been thrust into living between two "universes." An often unseen guide had helped him survive the perils of each, appearing at the appropriate time in the form of the Yaqui elder.

For now, Charlie's body and mind had to express the essence of the Spiritual realm in the world of forms. And in front of him stood the man who had carried his mind, and perhaps his spirit, into the very depths of hell.

Wentworth could not be blamed for all of this. Could a man be blamed for being possessed by the Devil, or a four centimeter square tumor that created psychotic behavior?

The war, in any case, was over. But it could not be forgotten, particularly by Charlie.

Wentworth knew that time was needed for mending. Charlie had not asked him to stay, and it was not his place to remain there uninvited. The once omnipotent industrialist walked down the hill toward an uncertain future. Whatever road he took would be hard, but honest.

Winter came, marked by Charlie and Emma's wedding and an expansion of the clinic. The guerrilla war raged on, but the Federales were realizing the futility of its continuation. Wentworth came to the clandestine Bacatete mountain village with some badly needed medical supplies. Emma insisted that he stay for supper. She and her father finally talked, while Charlie listened. Carlos spent the night with the curanderos. Wentworth left in the morning.

With the coming of spring, and the Fiesta del Gloria, Wentworth was invited to stay for Holy Week. Charlie and Wentworth talked, Emma listened. Carlos watched from the curanderos' window.

The fall was marked by a truce with the Federales and Charlie's invitation for Wentworth to meet his grandson. The visit lasted for twenty years.

ABOUT THE AUTHOR

M. J. Politis holds a Ph.D. in human physiology, a D.V.M. in veterinary medicine and the H.B.A.R.P. degree (Human Being, Aspiring Renaissance Person).

His other writing credits include made-for-TV movies, plays, and a series of innovative "how-to" books/scripts, which use comedy and drama to drive home biomedical technical information. He has over fifty original scientific publication credits, in areas ranging from toxicology to reconstructive neurology. More recently, he was co-author of *The Complete Idiot's Guide to Increasing Your Intelligence* (published by MacMillan).

He is also an avid horseman and real-life part-time veterinarian.

Born, raised and educated in New York, he is currently living in Western Canada.